YouTube 4 You

Michael Miller

D1448474

que

YouTube 4 You

Copyright © 2007 by Que Publishing

International Standard Book Number 0-7897-3698-5

Printed in the United States of America

First Printing: May 2007

10   09   08   07   4   3   2   1

Library of Congress Cataloging-in-Publication Data:

Miller, Michael, 1958-
  YouTube 4 You / Michael Miller.
      p. cm.
  Includes index.
  ISBN 0-7897-3698-5
  1. YouTube (Electronic resource) 2. Internet videos. 3. Online social networks. 4. YouTube (Firm) I. Title. II. Title: YouTube for you.
  TK5105.8867.M45 2007
  006.7--dc22

                                             2007010930

Trademarks

Warning and Disclaimer

Bulk Sales

Que Publishing offers excellent discounts o[n this book when ordered] in quantity for bulk purchases or special sal[es.] please contact

> **U.S. Corporate and Government** [Sales]
> **1-800-382-3419**
> **corpsales@pearsontechgroup.co[m]**

For sales outside the United States, please c[ontact]

> **International Sales**
> **international@pearsoned.com**

Associate Publisher
Greg Wiegand

Acquisitions Editor
Michelle Newcomb

Development Editor
Kevin Howard

Technical Editor
Vince Averello

Managing Editor
Gina Kanouse

Senior Project Editor
Lori Lyons

Copy Editor
Geneil Breeze

Proofreader
Paula Lowell

Indexer
Erika Millen

Publishing Coordinator
Cindy Teeters

Interior Designer
Anne Jones

Cover Designer
Anne Jones

Contents at a Glance

This Book Is Safari Enabled

The Safari® Enabled icon on the cover of your favorite technology book means the book is available through Safari Bookshelf.

When you buy this book, you get free access to the online edition for 45 days.

Safari Bookshelf is an electronic reference library that lets you easily search thousands of technical books, find code samples, download chapters,and access technical information whenever and wherever you need it.

To gain 45-day Safari Enabled access to this book:

- Go to http://www.quepublishing.com/safarienabled
- Complete the brief registration form
- Enter the coupon code EYQA-QHTQ-UAPK-V4P6-6BC1

If you have difficulty registering on Safari Bookshelf or accessing the online edition, please e-mail customer service@safaribooksonline.com.

Table of Contents

VIII

About the Author

Michael Miller has written more than 75 nonfiction how-to books in the past two decades, including Que's *Googlepedia: The Ultimate Google Resource, iPodpedia: The Ultimate iPod and iTunes Resource, Absolute Beginner's Guide to Computer Basics, Absolute Beginner's Guide to eBay,* and *How Microsoft Windows Vista Works.* He also writes about digital lifestyle topics for a number of websites.

Mr. Miller has established a reputation for clearly explaining technical topics to nontechnical readers, and for offering useful real-world advice about complicated topics. More information can be found at the author's website, located at www.molehillgroup.com.

Dedication

To Sherry, as always.

Acknowledgments

Thanks to the usual suspects at Que Publishing, including but not limited to Greg Wiegand, Michelle Newcomb, Kevin Howard, Anne Jones, Lori Lyons, Geneil Breeze, Erika Millen, Kim Scott, and Paula Carroll.

We Want to Hear from You!

As the reader of this book, *you* are our most important critic and commentator. We value your opinion and want to know what we're doing right, what we could do better, what areas you'd like to see us publish in, and any other words of wisdom you're willing to pass our way.

As an executive editor for Que Publishing, I welcome your comments. You can email or write me directly to let me know what you did or didn't like about this book—as well as what we can do to make our books better.

Please note that I cannot help you with technical problems related to the topic of this book. We do have a User Services group, however, where I will forward specific technical questions related to the book.

When you write, please be sure to include this book's title and author as well as your name, email address, and phone number. I will carefully review your comments and share them with the author and editors who worked on the book.

Email: feedback@quepublishing.com

Mail: Michelle Newcomb
Acquisitions Editor
Que Publishing
800 East 96th Street
Indianapolis, IN 46240 USA

For more information about this book or another Que Publishing title, visit our website at www.quepublishing.com. Type the ISBN (excluding hyphens) or the title of a book in the Search field to find the page you're looking for.

Introduction

YouTube is greatest thing since sliced bread.

No, really. I mean, how many other websites suck you in like YouTube does? YouTube has to be biggest time waster on the Internet. You start watching one video, then click to another, and before you know it you've spent an entire evening clicking and viewing, clicking and viewing.

What's cool is just how much different stuff is on YouTube. For example, I'm a big jazz fan; I can't get over how many classic jazz clips are available to watch—Miles Davis, the Dave Brubeck Quartet, you name it. I also like watching old toy commercials from when I was a kid (yay, Major Matt Mason!), and YouTube never disappoints. Then there are all those clips from recent television broadcasts, and the latest viral videos. Is there no end to what's available on YouTube?

That's why YouTube has become one of the most-visited sites on the web in such a short period of time. Whatever you're interested in, there's something to watch. And, if that isn't enough, you can always upload your own videos to the site to share with anyone who cares to watch. YouTube is a not just a video *watching* community, it's also a video *sharing* community.

In fact, there's a lot of community on the YouTube site—much more than you might know about if all you do is watch an occasional video. For example, did you know that you can email links to your favorite videos to your friends and family? Or create discussion groups centered on specific types of videos? Or embed YouTube videos in your own blog or web page?

That's right, there's a lot you probably don't know about YouTube—yet. That's because you're still reading the introduction to this book. Turn a few pages, and *YouTube 4 You* will tell you all about these cool features (and more), and how to use them. If it's available on the YouTube site, you'll learn about it here. Promise.

How This Book Is Organized

YouTube 4 You is a quick read that contains a lot of information about YouTube's various and sundry features. To make finding that job easier, this book is organized into four main parts, each focused on a particular type of YouTuber:

- **Part I, "YouTube 4 Everyone,"** provides an introduction to YouTube—how it all started, and where everything is located on the YouTube site.

- **Part II, "YouTube 4 Viewers,"** tells you how to find and view videos on the YouTube site. You'll also learn how to manage and share links to your favorite videos, and even how to download YouTube videos to your PC or iPod.

- **Part III, "YouTube 4 Video Makers,"** shows you how to create videos for sharing on YouTube. You'll learn what makes a great YouTube video, what file formats and resolution to use, how to upload and manage your videos, and how to deal with various legal issues—including copyright violations.

- **Part IV, "YouTube 4 Advanced Users,"** is for anyone who wants to take YouTube to the next level. You'll learn how to work within the YouTube community, customize your own channel profile, add YouTube videos to your website or blog, make money from your YouTube videos, and troubleshoot YouTube problems.

Although I recommend reading the book in consecutive order, you don't have to. Read it in chapter order if you want (I think it flows fairly well as written), or read just those chapters that interest you—kind of like jumping around from one YouTube video to another. I won't get upset if you don't read the whole thing.

Conventions Used in This Book

I hope that this book is easy enough to figure out on its own, without requiring its own instruction manual. As you read through the pages, however, it helps to know precisely how I've presented specific types of information.

Menu Commands

Although this book is about YouTube proper, sometimes that involves talking about web browsers and other pieces of software. To indicate navigation through software programs, I use the following notation:

Main menu, Submenu, Submenu.

All you have to do is follow the instructions in order, using your mouse to click through the various menus and submenus. For example, if I tell you to select Tools, Internet Options in Internet Explorer, you know to pull down the Tools menu and select Internet Options. It's pretty easy.

Web Pages

Obviously, there are lots of web page addresses in the book, like this one: www.youtube.com. When you see one of these addresses (also known as a *URL*), you can go to that web page by entering the URL into the address box in your web browser. I've made every effort to ensure the accuracy of the web addresses presented here, but given the ever-changing nature of the Web, don't be surprised if you run across a few addresses that have changed. I apologize in advance.

Special Elements

As you read through this book you'll note several special elements, presented in what we in the publishing business call "margin notes." There are different types of margin notes for different types of information, as you see here.

 This is a note that presents some interesting information, even if it isn't wholly relevant to the discussion in the main text.

Tip 4U This is a tip that might prove useful for whatever you're in the process of doing.

Warning 4U This is a warning that something you might accidentally do might have undesirable results—so take care!

There's More on the Web

Now that you know how to use this book, it's time to get to the heart of the matter. But when you're ready to take a break from viewing YouTube videos, browse over to my blog for this book, **YouTube 4U: The Blog** (youtube4u.blogspot.com). Here you'll find more information about YouTube, including new features added since this book was printed. I'll also post any updates or corrections to this book, in the inevitable event that an error or two creeps into this text. (Hey, nobody's perfect!)

While you're on the web, you may also want to check out my personal website, located at www.molehillgroup.com. Here you'll find more information about all the other books I've written and am in the process of writing. You never know—you might find something else worth reading.

In addition, know that I love to hear from readers of my books. If you want to contact me, feel free to email me at youtube@ molehillgroup.com. I can't promise that I'll answer every message, but I do promise that I'll read each one!

But enough with the preliminaries. Turn the page and start YouTubing!

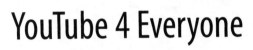

YouTube 4 Everyone

1

Welcome to YouTube

You've been there. You've seen it. You know that YouTube is hot—because it's cool. That's why you like it.

But what makes YouTube so cool—and so hot? It's all about videos, and about sharing them.

YouTube—Video Sharing 4 Everyone

YouTube's motto is "Broadcast Yourself." (It's there in the logo, as you can see in Figure 1.1.) Technically, that means YouTube is a video sharing site that lets users upload and view all sorts of video clips online. The site has become a repository for literally millions of movie clips, TV clips (both current and classic), music videos, and home videos. The most popular YouTube videos quickly become "viral," getting passed around from email to email and linked to from other sites and blogs on the web. If a YouTube video is particularly interesting, you'll see it pop up virtually everywhere, from TV's *The Daily Show* to the front page of your favorite website.

Figure 1.1
YouTube's motto: Broadcast Yourself. (It's trademarked!)

All of those videos and all of that sharing make YouTube one of the hottest sites on the Internet today—and one of the largest and fastest-growing. According to Nielsen/NetRatings, YouTube consistently ranks in the top 10 of all websites, with close to 20 million visitors per month. And those visitors are watching a lot of videos; *USA Today* reports that more than 100 million clips are viewed on the site each day, with more than 65,000 new videos uploaded every 24 hours.

What makes YouTube so appealing? Most users would say, "the videos." But how do those videos get there? It's the sharing aspect of the site that defines its success; YouTube visitors can both consume and contribute the videos that make up the site.

And whether you're watching or uploading those videos, YouTube is an easy site to use. Finding a video is as easy as searching or browsing; watching a video requires nothing more than the click of a Play button; and uploading a video isn't much more difficult than attaching a file to an email message. The site itself does all the heavy lifting in terms of technology—the conversion of uploaded videos to a standard format, the provision of necessary hard disk space and bandwidth to host the videos, and the serving of the videos at the push of the proverbial button. YouTube even lets you send links to its videos to your friends and family via email, and host those links on your own website or blog. And it's all extraordinarily easy.

Info 4U In April 2005, *Forbes* magazine estimated that YouTube consumed 200 terabytes of bandwidth per day—easily costing more than $1 million per month. That was when the site had half the traffic it currently has; figure at least double those numbers today.

So whether you like to watch or like to share, YouTube gives you what you want, the way you want it. That's why it's so successful.

How It All Started: The History of YouTube

YouTube is so pervasive and so innovative that it was named Invention of the Year by *Time* magazine in 2006. That's not too bad for a site that first came to life only the year before.

YouTube was conceived by three former employees of PayPal—Chad Hurley, Steven Chen, and Jawed Karim. With some PayPal bucks in their pockets, the three friends were looking for a new business opportunity and realized that there was a real need for a service that facilitated the process of uploading, watching, and sharing videos. Hence the development of YouTube.

The trio registered the domain name YouTube.com on February 15, 2005, and then started developing the technology for the site—in Hurley's garage. Chen, the programmer of the bunch, worked with Adobe's Flash development language to stream video clips inside a web browser. Hurley, a user interface expert, adopted the concept of "tags" to let users identify and share the videos they liked. Together, they came up with a way to let users paste video clips onto their own web pages (and, most importantly, on their MySpace pages), which expanded the reach the site.

The development work done, a public beta test version of the site went live in May 2005. After a few months of working the kinks out of the site, YouTube was officially launched in December 2005.

That's when things really started cooking.

The three former "PayPals" had done their homework; the site proved immensely popular from virtually the first day in business. As you can see in Figure 1.2, site traffic that first month was 3 million visitors, which is pretty good for a startup. The number of visitors tripled by the third month (February), tripled again by July (to 30 million visitors), and reached 38 million visitors by the end of the site's first year in business. That made YouTube one of the top 10 sites on the web, period—and one of the fastest-growing websites in history.

That kind of growth didn't escape the notice of the big boys. In fact, one of the biggest boys in the dot-com biz decided that YouTube was ripe for the taking; in October 2006, Google acquired YouTube, paying $1.65 billion in Google stock. That made for a nice little payday for YouTube's founding fathers.

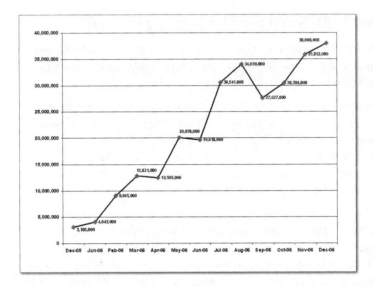

Figure 1.2
YouTube unique visitors per month, as reported by Nielsen/NetRatings (www.nielsen-netratings.com).

Even though YouTube is now part of the Google conglomerate, the site continues to operate independently. That's a good thing for YouTube users; the site looks and acts the same today as it did in the pre-Google days.

Today, YouTube has about 70 employees; Chad Hurley is CEO (chief executive officer) and Steven Chen is CTO (chief technical officer). The company's main offices are in San Mateo, California.

And, you might ask, how does YouTube make money—especially because it's totally free to both watch and upload videos? YouTube's revenues come the old-fashioned way—by selling advertising on the site. Interestingly, the site didn't generate much revenue before it was purchased by Google; Google's advertising services were a big help to YouTube, adding targeted banner ads to the site. This is one instance where an acquisition truly added value to the company being acquired!

 Co-founder Jawed Karim left YouTube in 2005 to pursue an advanced degree at Stanford University.

Videos, Videos, and More Videos: What's On YouTube

What can you find on the YouTube site? It's safe to say that just about any kind of video you're interested in, YouTube has it—or something like it.

Many videos on YouTube are the Internet equivalent of *America's Funniest Home Videos*, amateur videos of everything from birthday parties to *Jackass*-style stunts. Anybody with a video camera can easily upload home movies to YouTube and make them available for the whole world to see.

Other videos on YouTube are decidedly more professional. Budding film professionals can post their work on YouTube, which essentially converts the site into a giant repository of filmmakers' resumes. Student films, independent videos, acting and directing tryouts—they're all there.

Then there is the category of "video blog," or *vlog*. This is a video version of the traditional text-based blog, a personal journal typically captured via webcam and posted to YouTube on a regular basis. Most video bloggers post new entries on a regular basis—or when they have something particularly interesting to say.

YouTube is also a repository for "historical" items. We're talking old television commercials, music videos, clips from classic television shows, you name it. Want to revisit your childhood and watch an old Maypo commercial? Several are on YouTube. How about a clip of the Ronettes performing on *Hullaballoo*? Or the Beatles on the *Ed Sullivan Show*? Or your favorite episode of the old *Speed Racer* cartoon? They're all there, believe it or not. YouTube is a great site for nostalgia buffs, collectors, and the like.

Speaking of music videos, there is no better site on the web to find your favorite video clips. In fact, YouTube has announced that it hopes to offer every music video ever created and is in talks with Warner Music Group, EMI, Universal Music Group, Sony BMG Music Entertainment, and other record labels to make this happen. That makes YouTube a great place to promote hot new music and bands. If you're a music lover, you'll love YouTube.

A lot of current television content is also on the YouTube site. Although not every television network agrees that YouTube is a valid promotional medium (meaning that some networks have asked YouTube to pull their content), many clips from popular TV shows are still on the site—plus movie trailers, promotional videos, and similar items. YouTube is a TV and movie lover's dream.

So what's on YouTube tonight? As you can see, a little bit of everything!

How YouTube Works

The seemingly simple serving of so many videos is actually a complex endeavor. It only looks easy.

Users upload videos to YouTube in either QuickTime, AVI, or MPEG file formats. YouTube then converts these video files into Flash FLV format—which is how the videos are served to YouTube users. (To view YouTube videos in your web browser, you must have Macromedia Flash Player—version 7 or later—installed.) All the videos are stored on YouTube's servers, which are hosted by Limelight Networks—a leading provider of content-hosting and streaming media solutions.

 YouTube uses Flash technology with the Sorenson Spark H.263 video codec. YouTube videos are recompressed at a lower bitrate than the original submissions so that they download and play faster for most viewers. Audio is mono.

When you access a YouTube video, the video begins streaming to your computer. When enough of the video has streamed to create a sufficient "buffer," playback begins.

Because YouTube utilizes streaming video technology, the file itself is not saved to your hard disk. That's because streaming video is different from downloading a complete video file. When you download a file, you can't start playing that file until it is completely downloaded to your PC. With streaming video, however, playback can start before an entire file is downloaded; the first part of the file is present on your PC while the last part is still downloading. It makes for almost-immediate video playback, especially if you have a broadband Internet connection—which means immediate gratification for YouTube viewers!

2

Getting Around the YouTube Site

Whether you want to watch someone else's videos or upload videos of your own, you need to know how to get around the YouTube site. It's a wild ride—with something interesting around every corner!

Navigating the Home Page

When you first access YouTube (www.youtube.com), you see the home page shown in Figure 2.1. This is your home base for the entire site; from here you can browse videos, search for videos, access your favorite videos, and even upload your own videos.

A lot of stuff is on this home page, including (pretty much in top-to-bottom order)

▓ Links to your account info, history of videos you've viewed, a QuickList of videos you've tagged for future viewing, and YouTube's help system

▓ A search box that lets you search for videos on the YouTube site

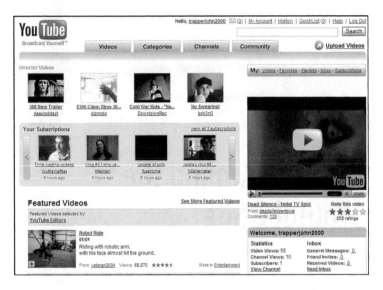

Figure 2.1
The YouTube home page.

- Tabs that let you access specific YouTube content—Videos, Categories, Channels, and Community
- A link that lets you upload your own videos
- A selection of Director Videos—videos from some of YouTube's most talented video makers
- The latest videos from those channels you've subscribed to
- Links to your (My) uploaded videos, favorite videos, video playlists, email inbox, and videos you've subscribed to
- A selection of Featured Videos—the hottest or coolest videos on YouTube today
- A specific featured video; click the Play button to begin playback
- Info about your account—how many times your uploaded videos have been viewed, how many email messages you've received, and so forth
- What's New at YouTube—the latest news about the YouTube site
- Popular Videos for Mobile Devices—videos specifically formatted for viewing on cell phones and other portable devices

- Active Channels—a selection of videos from the most active current YouTube channels
- Active Groups—a selection of videos from the most active YouTube groups

 We'll discuss YouTube groups and channels in Chapter 12, "Joining the YouTube Community—And Creating Your Own Channel."

Finally, at the bottom of the home page, you'll find links to other essential site features—Your Account information, Help & Info pages, and YouTube company information.

Exploring YouTube's Content Tabs

As you'll learn in Chapter 3, "Finding Videos to Watch," you can find videos on YouTube by searching (using the top-of-page Search box) or by browsing. Most of the browsing is done using the tabs near the top of the YouTube home page—so let's see what you'll find on each one.

Videos

Click the Videos tab and you're taken to a page full of videos, such as the one shown in Figure 2.2, with links to various types of videos along the left side. The four categories of links include

- **Browse**—Most Recent, Most Viewed, Top Rated, Most Discussed, Top Favorites, Most Linked, Recently Featured, Most Responded, Watch on Mobile, and Supervote Gallery
- **Time**—Today, This Week, This Month, or All Time
- **Category**—All, Arts & Animation, Autos & Vehicles, Comedy, Entertainment, Music, News & Blogs, People, Pets & Animals, Science & Technology, Sports, Travel & Places, and Video Games
- **Language**—All, English, Spanish, Japanese, German, Chinese, and French

Click a Browse, Time, Category, or Language link to see all the videos of that type.

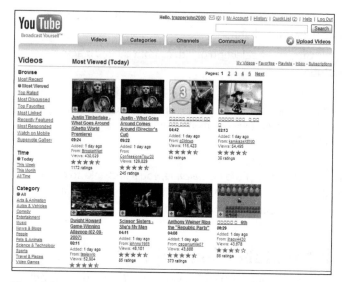

Figure 2.2
Browsing videos on the Videos tab.

Categories

Click the Categories tab and you see a list of featured videos by category (Figure 2.3), along with links to the full categories on the left side. Click the See More links to view more videos within each category.

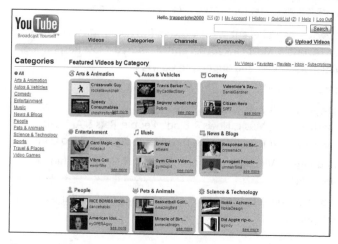

Figure 2.3
Viewing featured videos on the Categories tab.

Channels

Click the Channels tab and you see the featured videos in the most-subscribed YouTube Channels, as shown in Figure 2.4. (A *channel* is a personal list of favorite and uploaded videos; every user can create her own channel.) On the left side of the page are links to the four main types of channels (Comedians, Directors, Musicians, and Partners), along with links for browsing the Most Recent, Most Viewed, and Most Subscribed channels, as well as channels posted This Week, This Month, or All Time.

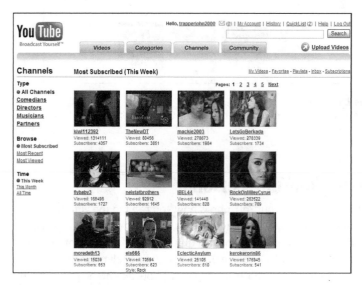

Figure 2.4
Viewing featured videos on the Channels tab.

Community

Click the Community tab and you see the featured videos by YouTube community—Groups, Contests, and Colleges, as shown in Figure 2.5. Click the See More link by each type of community to see more of the same.

Figure 2.5
Viewing videos from groups, contests, and colleges on the Community tab.

Making YouTube Personal

One neat thing about YouTube is how you can tag the videos you like for future viewing—via a Favorites list, customized video playlists, and so on. YouTube also provides quick links to key account information, including videos you've uploaded. Links to all these lists and information are located at the top of the YouTube home page and in the My section just below the tabs. Here's what you'll find when you click these links:

- **My Videos**—In the My box, takes you to a list of videos you've uploaded to YouTube

- **My Favorites**— In the My box, takes you to a list of videos you've tagged as your favorites

- **My Playlists**—In the My box, takes you to a list of video playlists you've created and the videos within each playlist

- **My Inbox**—In the My box, takes you to YouTube's email and message center

- **My Subscriptions**—In the My box, shows all the video channels you've subscribed to

- **My Account**—At the top of the page, takes you to your account management page, where you can edit account information, your subscriptions and groups, and so on

- **History**—At the top of the page, displays the most-recent videos you've viewed

- **QuickList**—At the top of the page, displays videos you've tagged for future viewing

- **Help**—At the top of the page, takes you to YouTube's help center

- **Log out**—At the top of the page, logs you out of your YouTube account

Uploading Videos

As you know, YouTube isn't just for viewing; you can also upload your own videos to the YouTube site. This is accomplished by clicking Upload Videos at the top right of the YouTube home page; this takes you to a series of pages that guide you through the video uploading process.

 Learn more about uploading videos in Chapter 9, "Uploading Videos to YouTube."

Wait! There's More!

Your guided tour of the YouTube site isn't over just yet. As you can see in Figure 2.6, a bunch of links are at the bottom of the YouTube home page, below a second Search box. The links are grouped into three sections:

Figure 2.6
Links at the bottom of YouTube's home page.

- **Your Account**—Links to your personal picks (Favorites, Playlists, and so on) and account information

- **Help & Info**—Links to YouTube's help center, Code of Conduct, and other site-related information and services

- **YouTube**—Links to information about YouTube, the company

Let's look at some of the most important of these individual links.

YouTube Blog

Click the Blog link in the YouTube section and you're taken to The YouTube Blog. As you can see in Figure 2.7, this is a text-and-video blog put together by YouTube's editors—it's a great way to meet the people behind the scenes, and learn more about YouTube in the process.

Figure 2.7
A typical post at the YouTube Blog.

Test Tube

Want to know more about upcoming YouTube features—new services that are currently works in process? Then click the Test Tube link in the YouTube section. This displays a list of features currently in the YouTube "incubator." For example, Figure 2.8 shows two new features—AudioSwap, for adding licensed music soundtracks to your videos; and Streams, for chatting with other video viewers in real time. Click the link to sign up to test a new TestTube feature.

Figure 2.8
Test new YouTube features on the TestTube page.

 YouTube's TestTube features are still in the development phase—which means that all the bugs probably aren't worked out of them yet.

Getting Help

Confused? Having problems? Need a hand? Then access YouTube's Help Center, shown in Figure 2.9. Just click the Help link at the top of YouTube's home page or the Help Center link at the bottom of any YouTube page. You can browse articles that guide you through various aspects of the YouTube experience—Getting Started; Making, Uploading, and Promoting Videos; The YouTube Community;

Account and Policies; and Troubleshooting. If you can't find an answer to your immediate question, use the Search Help Center box to search through all available Help Center topics.

If you're still perplexed, you can ask the folks at YouTube for assistance. Point your web browser at www.youtube.com/contact to access the Contact Us page, enter your email address and question, and then click the Send Message button. Someone from YouTube should respond to you within a day or two.

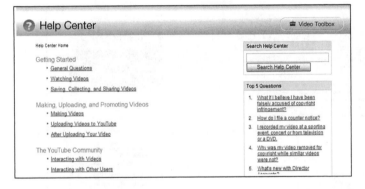

Figure 2.9
The YouTube Help Center.

Joining YouTube

To take full advantage of YouTube's features, you need to set up your own personal YouTube account. Naturally, you must have an account before you can upload any videos to the site. But you also need an account to save your favorite videos, create playlists, join groups and communities, and so on.

Fortunately, it's both easy and free to create a YouTube account. Just go to the home page, scroll to the Member Login box, and then click the Sign Up link. YouTube displays the Join YouTube page, shown in Figure 2.10. Select an Account Type (for most users, a Standard account is the way to go) and then enter the appropriate personal information—email address, desired username, desired password, country where you live, postal code, gender, and date of birth. Click the Sign Up button and YouTube will send a confirmation message to your email address; click the link in that email message to confirm your subscription.

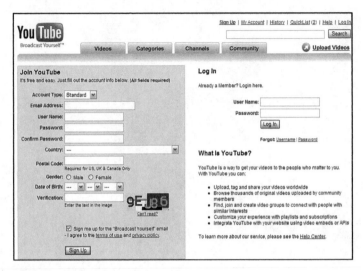

Figure 2.10
Signing up for a YouTube account.

After you're in, you need to log in to YouTube to use your account. Do this by clicking the Log In link at the top of the YouTube home page; enter your username and password, and you're ready to start viewing!

YouTube 4 Viewers

3

Finding Videos to Watch

With millions and millions of videos available on YouTube, how do you find the ones you want to watch? Well, finding videos on YouTube is a lot like finding stuff on the web—you can browse for it, or you can search for it. It's really quite easy.

Browsing for Videos

Most new users start out by browsing YouTube for interesting videos. Browsing is perhaps the best way to discover new videos; you can click through the categories until you find something you like.

How to Browse

Browsing YouTube is a simple matter of clicking a link—and then another link, and then another link, and then another link. The more you click, the more you discover.

 Actually, many people are introduced to YouTube when they're sent a link to a particularly interesting video. If you receive such an email, just click the enclosed link; this will take you to the YouTube page for that video, and playback should start automatically.

For example, when you choose to browse by category (which we'll discuss in a moment), you start by clicking the Categories tab on the YouTube home page. This takes you to the Categories page, shown in Figure 3.1. On this page you click a link for a particular category—Music, for example. This displays a page of featured videos in the Music category, as shown in Figure 3.2. To view an individual video on this page, just click the video.

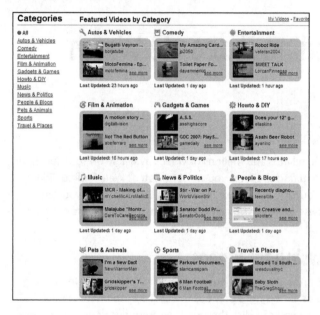

Figure 3.1
Browsing YouTube via the Categories page.

The only problem with browsing is that you don't get to see everything that's available. Instead, you're browsing a list of featured videos in that category, as selected by the YouTube staff. Still, it's a good way to explore what's available—and to see the best of the best.

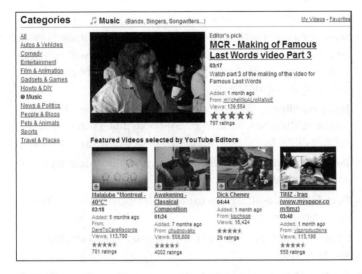

Figure 3.2
Browsing featured videos in the Music category.

Browsing by Category

For most users, the best way to browse YouTube is by category. You do this by clicking the Categories tab.

YouTube organizes its videos into the following major categories:

- **Autos & Vehicles**—The place for videos about planes, trains, and automobiles—car chases, monster truck rallies, flight films, you name it

- **Comedy**—Home of the funniest stuff on YouTube, from amateur video high jinks to stand-up comedy routines to clips from movie comedies

- **Entertainment**—A hodgepodge of short movies, odd stuff, and other random entertainment

- **Film & Animation**—Where you find classic cartoons, animated shorts, computer-generated animation, short art films, and the like

- **Gadgets & Games**—The category for all sorts of technology products, video game hints and reviews, and the like

- **Howto & DIY**—Home for online instruction and training videos

- **Music**—One of YouTube's biggest categories, full of music videos and classic performance clips from major artists, as well as performances from amateur and up-and-coming musicians and user-compiled music montages

- **News & Politics**—Where you'll find the most newsworthy clips on the YouTube site, including stories from professional news organizations, live events captured by video cameras, and more

- **People & Blogs**—A combination of funny home videos and personal video blogs

- **Pets & Animals**—The place to find both Stupid Pet Tricks and cute animal videos

- **Sports**—A vast repository of both professional and amateur sports highlights

- **Travel & Places**—The place to find homemade travel videos and neat nature clips

The main Categories page lists two featured videos for each category, which you can click to view directly. To view all the videos in a category, click the category link on the left side of the page or the See More link in the category box in the middle of the page. Click that link and you'll see a list of the featured videos for that category.

Browsing by Channel

Browsing by category isn't the only way to see what YouTube has to offer. YouTube also organizes videos by *channel*, which is a great way to find videos by people whose tastes you share.

A channel is simply a personal collection of videos by a specific YouTube user. Every YouTube user has his own channel. You might not know it, but you even have *your* own channel—those videos you've saved as favorites as well as any videos of your own that you've uploaded.

To browse YouTube's featured channels, click the Channels tab on the YouTube home page. From here you can browse the following types of channels:

- **All Channels**—Doesn't actually list every YouTube user, but instead displays the most-subscribed-to channels

- **Comedians**—Lists channels by users who sign up for YouTube in the Comedian category, typically professional comedians, makers of funny short films, and the like

- **Directors**—Lists channels by users who sign up for YouTube in the Directors category, typically amateur or independent film directors showing their wares on the YouTube site

- **Gurus**—Lists channels offerered by experts on specific topics

- **Musicians**—Lists channels by users who sign up for YouTube in the Musicians category, typically professional or amateur musicians who upload their own performance clips or music videos

- **Partners**—Displays channels by YouTube's commercial partners: Adult Swim, BBC, BBC Worldwide, Beggars Group, Capitol Records, CBS, Charlie Rose, Fox News Blast, G4TV, Game-Trailers.com, GSN (The Games Network), NBA, NBC Entertainment, Nettwerk Music, NHL, PBS, Playboy, Showtime, Sony BMG, SpikeTV, Sony Pictures Classics, SubPop Records, Sundance Channel, TNA Wrestling, TVT Records, Universal Music Group, VH1, Warner Music Group, We Put Out Records, and more

- **Politicians**—Lists channels maintained by major presidential candidates

 You can access any user's channel page by clicking the user's name underneath a video, comment, message, or other item.

When you click a channel link, you see that user's channel page. Channel pages can be simple (such as the author's own channel shown in Figure 3.3) or professionally designed (such as the partner channel shown in Figure 3.4).

On a simple channel page, there are links at the top to view more from this user—the user's own uploaded videos, favorites, playlists, groups, friends, subscribers, and subscriptions. Click the Playlists link, for example, to view the playlists that this user has created; click the Subscriptions link to view which groups this user has subscribed to, and so on.

Figure 3.3
A typical user channel page.

Figure 3.4
A professional channel page by a YouTube partner—in this case, CBS.

If you like the videos from this particular user or partner, you can sub-scribe to her channel. When you subscribe to a channel, you'll be notified of new videos uploaded by this user. To subscribe, simply click the Subscribe button near the top of the user's channel page.

 Learn more about channels, subscriptions, and the like in Chapter 12, "Joining the YouTube Community—And Creating Your Own Channel."

Browsing the Most Popular Videos

Another fun way to browse YouTube is to journey through the most popular videos on the site. This is a great way to find the latest *viral videos*—those videos that are taking the web by storm.

There are several ways to browse YouTube's top videos—all dependent on how you define "top" or "most popular." Here's what you can do:

- To see the top picks from the YouTube staff, simply examine the featured videos on the YouTube home page, or, to view recent staff picks, select the Videos tab and click the Recently Featured link.

- To see the most-viewed videos today, select the Videos tab and click the Most Viewed link.

- To see the top-rated videos (videos that other users thought were the best), select the Videos tab and click the Top Rated link.

- To see the videos that generated the most discussion among other users, select the Videos tab and click the Most Discussed links.

- To see the videos that were most often selected as user favorites, select the Videos tab and click the Top Favorites link.

- To see the videos that were most linked to from sites outside YouTube, select the Videos tab and click the Most Linked link.

- To see the videos that garnered the most user responses, select the Videos tab and click the Most Responded link.

Within any category or type of video, you can view the newest videos by clicking one of the links in the Time section on the left side of the page—Today, This Week, This Month, or All Time.

Searching for Videos

When you're not sure what you want to watch, browsing by category or popularity is probably the way to go. If you have a particular type of video in mind, however, searching is a better approach.

 You can also search YouTube from the Google Video (video.google.com) site. Any Google Video search returns primarily YouTube videos—another benefit of Google's owning YouTube!

Conducting a Search

Searching YouTube is easy. Search boxes, like the one shown in Figure 3.5, are located at the top and bottom of every YouTube page. (It's the same search box, just in different locations.) To search for a video, simply enter into this search box a keyword or two that describes what you're searching for and then click the Search button.

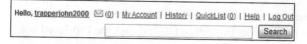

Figure 3.5
The YouTube Search box.

For example, if you want to search for Bruce Springsteen videos, enter **bruce springsteen** in the Search box. (Capitalization isn't necessary.) To search for clips of dancing monkeys, enter **dancing monkey**, and so on.

Working with Search Results

When you click the Search button, YouTube returns a list of videos that best match your search criteria, such as the one shown in

Figure 3.6. If you see a video you want to watch, just click it. Otherwise, you can narrow down a large list by using the links on the left side of the search results page:

- **Search In**—Restricts your search to only Videos (default), Channels, Groups, or Playlists

- **Sort By**—Sorts your results by Relevance (default), Date Added, View Count, or Rating

- **Refine by Category**—Lists only those results in the selected category

Figure 3.6
The results of a YouTube search.

So, for example, if you want to limit your search to the newest channels in the Comedy category, you would click Channels, Date Added, and then Comedy from the search results page.

Each search result contains the following information:

- Opening frame from the video

- Title of the video

- Total length of the video, in minutes and seconds

- A short description of the video
- Tags for the video—keywords that describe the video's content (click a tag to see more videos that have the same tag)
- When the video was added to YouTube
- Which category the video resides in
- The user who uploaded the video (click the user's name to see all videos in his channel)
- Number of times the video has been viewed
- Star rating of the video (The rating is from one to five stars— more is better.)
- The number of total ratings of this video

 See a video you want to watch, but can't watch right now? Then click the "+" sign at the bottom left of the video thumbnail; this adds the video to your QuickList. You can then click the QuickList link at the top of any YouTube page to revisit these flagged videos.

Finding Out About New Videos

YouTube video fans are constantly on the lookout for the latest, greatest, and coolest YouTube videos. But short of searching the YouTube site on a daily basis, how do you find out about the newest videos that might interest you?

The trick is in converting YouTube searches into RSS feeds. If you're familiar with blogs, you're familiar with feeds; these are constantly updated lists of new posts to a blog, to which users can subscribe. A feed subscription uses Real Simple Syndication (RSS) technology to notify subscribers of all new posts.

What most users don't know (yet) is that YouTube serves its searches as RSS feeds. All you have to do is create an RSS feed URL from the keyword of a YouTube search; you then add the feed URL to a feed reader program or feed aggregator website. Here's how it works.

First, find a tag that describes the type of video you're looking for. For example, if you're looking for new Beatles clips, the tag would be

beatles. If you're looking for new clips about the U.S. space program, the tag might be **nasa**. Then you use this tag to create a feed URL, like this:

```
http://www.youtube.com/rss/tag/tagname.rss
```

For example, to create a feed for those Beatles clips, you create the following URL:

```
http://www.youtube.com/rss/tag/beatles.rss
```

And the URL for the NASA feed looks like this:

```
http://www.youtube.com/rss/tag/nasa.rss
```

If you're searching on two or more tags, add them to the URL but leave a space between them. For example, to search for clips of Gnarls Barkley, use this URL:

```
http://www.youtube.com/rss/tag/gnarls barkley.rss
```

Add this URL to your feed reader or feed aggregator, and you'll be notified whenever new videos that match this search appear on the YouTube site.

 Some of the most popular feed reader programs include FeedDemon (www.feeddemon.com) and Feedreader (www.feedreader.com). Popular feed aggregator sites include Bloglines (www.bloglines.com), Google Reader (reader.google.com), and NewsGator (www.newsgator.com).

4

Watching YouTube Videos

The whole point of browsing or searching for videos on YouTube is to find a video to watch. Watching videos is what YouTube is all about, after all.

The nice thing about watching YouTube videos is that they play back in your web browser; no additional software is necessary, save for the Flash plugin for your browser. So get comfortable in front of your computer screen and get ready to watch!

Viewing the Video Page

When you click the title or thumbnail of any video on a search or browse page, a page for that video is displayed, like the one shown in Figure 4.1. This page has several sections, including the following:

- **Video player**—Where you watch the videos
- **Options**—For sharing and remembering this video
- **Information**—Key facts about the video
- **Related videos**—A great way to explore similar videos
- **Comments and responses**—What other users think about this video

We'll examine each section of this page in turn.

Figure 4.1
A YouTube video page.

Using the Video Player

The most important part of the video page is the video player; this is where the video plays back. In fact, playback is automatic—the video starts playing almost immediately after you open the video's page.

 Some large videos or videos played over a slow Internet connection may pause periodically after playback has started. This is due to the playback getting ahead of the streaming video download. If you find a video stopping and starting, just click the Play/Pause button to pause playback until more of the video has downloaded.

The video itself displays in the main video player window, as shown in Figure 4.2. The playback controls are located directly underneath the main window. From left to right, you use these controls to

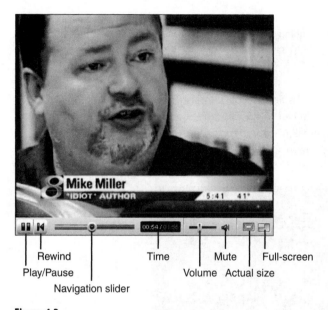

Figure 4.2
The YouTube video player.

- Pause playback by clicking the Play/Pause button; to resume playback, click the Play/Pause button again.
- Return to the start of the video by clicking the Rewind button.
- Navigate anywhere within the video by using the slider control. (This control also indicates how much of the video has downloaded; the slider fills with red as the video stream downloads.)
- View the elapsed and total time for the video via the time display.
- Control the sound level with the volume slider.
- Immediately mute the sound by clicking the Mute button.
- Display the video at its original size (often smaller than the window in your web browser) by clicking the first size button.
- Display the video in a full-screen window by clicking the second size button.

To watch a video within your web browser, you don't have to do anything other than open the video page. To view the video full-screen (instead of in the browser window) click the Full-screen button at the bottom right of the video player.

When a video is finished playing, YouTube displays a screen like the one shown in Figure 4.3. Click the Share button to send a link to this video via email to your friends. Click the Watch Again button to replay the video. Or click one of the other video links to watch a related video.

Figure 4.3
What you see when a video is finished playing.

Choosing Video Options

Directly below the video player is a box full of video options. This box offers some interesting information and lets you use the video in various ways:

- **Rate This Video**—Move your cursor across the stars to rate the video from one to five (the more stars the better).

- **Save to Favorites**—Click here to save this video in your YouTube Favorites list.

- **Add to Groups**—Click here to add this video to any group you currently belong to.

- **Share Video**—Click here to send a link to this video via email to friends and family.

- **Post Video**—Click here to post this video to a blog. (Assuming you have YouTube configured for your particular blog—see Chapter 13, "Adding YouTube Videos to Your Own Site or Blog," for more details.) You can also use this section to post a link to the video at a number of social networking sites, such as Digg, Del.icio.us, and StumbleUpon.

- **Flag as Inappropriate**—Click here to tell YouTube that something's not acceptable about this video (sexually explicit, mature content, graphic violence, hate speech, or other Terms of Use violation).

- **Views**—How many times this video has been viewed.

- **Comments**—How many viewers have commented on this video.

- **Favorited**—How many viewers have added this video to their Favorites list.

- **Honors**—For some particularly worthy videos, the web honors the video has received.

- **Links**—For some popular videos, a list of sites that link to the video.

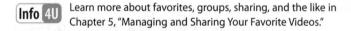 Learn more about favorites, groups, sharing, and the like in Chapter 5, "Managing and Sharing Your Favorite Videos."

Viewing Video Information

To the right of the video player is a box with specific information about this video. This box also includes a Subscribe button; click this button to subscribe to all videos posted by this particular user.

 Learn more about subscriptions in Chapter 12, "Joining the YouTube Community—And Creating Your Own Channel."

The other information in this box includes

- When the video was added to YouTube
- The name of the user who added the video

Click the user's name to view her YouTube channel—which includes other videos the user has uploaded.

- A brief description of the video
- The category the clip is in
- The video's tags—keywords used to describe the video
- The web page URL for this video; copy and paste this URL into your own web page or blog to link back to the video
- The HTML code necessary to embed the video in a separate web page or blog; copy and paste this code into your own page to display the video on your website

Exploring Related Videos

Below the video information box is a series of three tabs, followed by a scrolling list of videos below. What you see in the scrolling list depends on which tab you select:

- **Related**—Displays videos in some way similar to this one
- **More from This User**—Displays other videos uploaded by the same user
- **Playlists**—Displays playlists that have something in common with this video

Whichever of these tabs you select, YouTube by default displays the first 20 related videos or playlists. Click the See All Videos link to view a search page filled with related videos; you can then filter these search results by category, date, and the like.

 One of the cool things about YouTube is how you're easily led from one video to another. Find one video that you like, and it's easy to discover similar videos via the Related list.

Reading and Posting Comments and Responses

On most video pages, the bottom left of the page is taken up by a series of viewer comments. Users can post their comments about any video; comments can be considered or just exclamatory ("Cool video!"), depending on the person doing the posting.

Next to each comment are two links. The Reply link lets you reply to that comment; the Spam link reports the comment (and the person who posted the comment) to YouTube as unwanted spam.

To add your own text-based comment, simply scroll to the bottom of the Comments & Responses section and use the Comment on This Video box, like the one shown in Figure 4.4. Enter your comments; then click the Post Comment button.

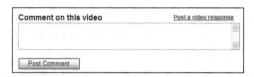

Figure 4.4
Posting a text comment about a video.

You can also post another video as a response to a video. To do this, click the Post a Video Response link; this displays the Video Response page shown in Figure 4.5. From here you can choose to record a video response (using a webcam and microphone), choose another video you've already uploaded to YouTube as your response, or upload a new video as your response. Follow the onscreen instructions to choose/upload the video you want to respond with.

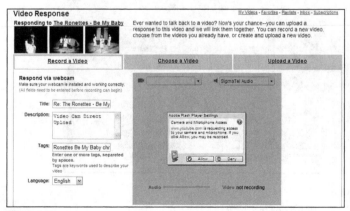

Figure 4.5
Recording a video response to a YouTube video.

Viewing Your Videos Full-Screen

By default, all YouTube videos display in the video player window in your web browser. If you would rather watch your videos larger, however, you can display any video in its own full-screen window.

 You may not want to watch all videos full-screen. Because most YouTube videos are optimized for the smaller video player, blowing them up to a larger size might make them too grainy or blocky to watch.

To view a video full-screen, click the Full-screen button at the bottom right of the YouTube video player. As you can see in Figure 4.6, this window functions as a freestanding video player, with the same transport controls underneath the video itself. You can maximize this window to appear full-screen on your computer desktop, or minimize the window to appear in a smaller sizeable window. Click the Close button in the lower-right corner to close this window and resume viewing the video in the normal browser-based video player.

Figure 4.6
Watching a video in a full-screen window.

Rating the Videos You Watch

Here's another cool thing about YouTube. You can give a rating to any video you've watched. Think a particular video is really hot? Give it a five-star rating. Think a video sucks wind? Then give it a one-star rating. Your voice will be heard.

To rate a video, all you have to do is drag your cursor across the stars beneath the YouTube video player in your web browser; stop your cursor over the star rating you want to give and then click your mouse. As you can see in Figure 4.7, you can give a video anywhere from one to five stars—the more stars, the higher the rating. After you've rated a video, your vote is added to the ratings given by other users to create an average rating. Thank you for voting!

Figure 4.7
Rating a YouTube video.

 To browse for the highest-rated videos, go to the Videos tab and then click the Top Rated link on the left side of the page.

Reporting Offensive Videos

There's one last thing to discuss when it comes to viewing videos. What do you do if you see a video that violates YouTube's content guidelines—a video that contains nudity or adult language? Well, YouTube is a self-policing community, which means it's your responsibility to report any offending videos you see. Then YouTube can check it out and, if necessary, remove the video from the site.

To report an offending video, click the Flag as Inappropriate link under the video player. This displays the box shown in Figure 4.8. Pull down the Choose a Reason list to tell YouTube what you find offensive about this video:

Figure 4.8
Reporting an offensive video.

- Sexually explicit
- Mature (over 18 only) content
- Other Terms of Use violation
- Graphic violence
- Hate speech

After making your selection, click the Flag This Video button. Your report is then forwarded to YouTube staffers, who will investigate the video in question and—if they agree with you—pull the video.

 Just because you report a video as offensive doesn't mean that YouTube will agree with you and pull the video. It's up to YouTube to make content-related decisions like this.

5

Managing and Sharing Your Favorite Videos

Watching videos on YouTube is great. But with so many videos to watch, how do you keep track of your favorites? And how do you share your favorite videos with others?

Actually, there are several ways to save your favorite videos for easier rewatching. And YouTube also makes it easy to share those videos with friends and family, via email. Read on to learn more.

Rewatching Recent Videos

Want to rewatch a video you've recently watched—but don't want to go through the whole browsing/searching process again? Then click the History link at the top of any YouTube page. This displays your Viewing History page, shown in Figure 5.1. Your most recently watched videos are listed here; just click a video to watch it again!

To clear your viewing history (in case you don't want friends or family seeing what you've watched), simply click the Clear Viewing History link at the bottom of the Viewing History page.

Figure 5.1
Reviewing your YouTube viewing history.

Flagging Videos for Future Viewing

Here's a familiar situation. You're browsing the YouTube site and find a video that looks interesting, but you don't have the time or inclination to watch it right then. Fortunately, YouTube lets you save this video in a temporary QuickList, without having to open the video page and start playback. Then, when you're ready, you can go back to this video and watch it at your leisure.

To add a video to your QuickList, all you have to do is click the little "+" button at the lower-left corner of any video thumbnail, as shown in Figure 5.2. Videos stay in your QuickList as long as your web browser is open; as soon as you close your browser window, the QuickList is flushed.

Figure 5.2
Click the "+" button to add this video to your QuickList for future viewing.

To see all the videos stored in your QuickList, click the QuickList link at the top of any YouTube page. This displays the QuickList page, shown in Figure 5.3. Click any video to view it, or click the Remove button to remove it from your QuickList (in case you decide you don't really want to watch it). You can even play all the videos in your QuickList one after another, by clicking the Play All Videos link.

Figure 5.3
Viewing videos in your QuickList.

YouTube also places a QuickList panel on all the video pages you open. This panel, shown in Figure 5.4, appears under the video player and above the normal options box. You can play videos directly from this panel, or click the Manage link to go to the main QuickList page. (If you would rather not see the QuickList panel, click the Hide button at the top right.)

Figure 5.4
The QuickList panel on a YouTube video page.

By default, videos remain in your QuickList after you've watched them. To remove videos after you've watched them, check the Remove Videos from QuickList as I Watch Them option on the QuickList page.

Saving Your Favorite Videos

When you view a video you really like, you don't want to forget about it. That's why YouTube lets you save your favorite videos in a Favorites list.

A YouTube Favorites list is kind of like the Favorites or Bookmarks list you have in your web browser. All your favorite videos are saved in a list that you can easily access for future viewing.

To save a video to your Favorites list, click the Save to Favorites link in the box beneath the YouTube video player. This displays the Add Video to Your Favorites pane, shown in Figure 5.5. Make sure the Favorites box is checked; then click OK. (You don't have to bother with the Add Video to a Playlist list—which we'll discuss next.)

Figure 5.5
Adding a video to your Favorites list.

When you want to revisit your favorite videos, go to the YouTube home page and click the Favorites link in the My box. As you can see in Figure 5.6, this displays a list of all your favorite videos. Click any video to watch it again.

 To delete a video from your Favorites list, simply check the box next to the video and then click the Remove Videos button.

Figure 5.6
The videos in your Favorites list.

Creating a Video Playlist

One of the challenges with YouTube is the sheer volume of videos available. Saving videos to your Favorites list is one way to manage this volume, but even your Favorites list can get too large to be easily manageable.

For that reason, you may want to create *playlists* separate from (or in addition to) your Favorites list. A YouTube playlist is simply a collection of videos, organized by whatever criteria you deem appropriate. You can play the videos in a playlist individually or as a group, just as you would the songs in a music playlist on your iPod. And, of course, YouTube lets you create multiple playlists, so you can have as many as you want.

Creating a Playlist from a Video Page

There are several ways to create a playlist and add a video to that playlist. The most common method is to open the page for that video and click the Save to Favorites link. When the Add Video to Your Favorites pane appears, pull down the Add Video to a Playlist list, select the playlist you want, and then click OK.

You don't have to add a video to your Favorites list to add it to a playlist; you can uncheck the Favorites option if you want.

If you haven't yet created a playlist, select [New Playlist] from the list and then click OK. This displays the Create/Edit Playlist page, shown in Figure 5.7. From here you have to enter some specific information about the new playlist:

Figure 5.7
Creating a new playlist.

- **Playlist Name**—The name you assign to the playlist
- **Video Log**—Check this option if you want this playlist used as the Video Log in your channel profile page
- **Description**—A short description of the contents of this playlist
- **Tags**—Optional keywords you can use to describe this playlist
- **Privacy**—Select whether this playlist should be public (for all YouTube users to view) or private (only you can view it)

 Learn more about channels and Video Logs in Chapter 12, "Joining the YouTube Community—And Creating Your Own Channel."

After you've filled in all the blanks, click the Save Playlist Info button. Your playlist is now saved.

Creating a Playlist from Your Favorites List

Another way to add a video to a playlist is from your Favorites list. Go to your Favorites page, check the video(s) you want to add, and then pull down the Copy Videos To list and select a playlist.

To create a new playlist from the Favorites page, click the Create Playlist button on the left side of the page. This opens the Create/Edit Playlist page; proceed as normal from there.

Alternatively, you can select those videos you want in the new playlist, then pull down the Copy Videos To list and select New Playlist. Again, this opens the Create/Edit Playlist page, this time with the selected videos already added.

Viewing Your Playlists

To view the playlists you've created, go to the YouTube home page and click the Playlists link in the My box. This displays the Playlists page, shown in Figure 5.8. All your playlists are listed at the left of the page; click a playlist name to see the videos in that playlist.

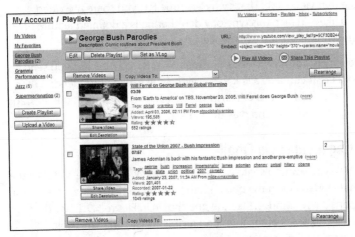

Figure 5.8
Viewing your YouTube playlists.

To play an individual video in a playlist, click that video. To play all the videos in a playlist one after another, click the Play All Videos link—or the big Play button next to the playlist name.

Editing Your Playlists

You can also use the Playlists page to edit your playlists:

■ To change the order of playback in a playlist, enter new numbers to the right of each video and then click the Rearrange button. The "1" video plays first, the "2" video plays second, and so on.

■ To remove a video from a playlist, check the small box to the left of the video and then click the Remove Videos button.

■ To set this playlist as the Video Log on your channel profile page, click the Set as VLog button.

■ To edit the title or description of a playlist, click the Edit button. This displays the Create/Edit Playlist page; proceed as normal from there.

■ To delete an entire playlist, click the Delete Playlist button.

Sharing Your Favorite Videos

If you like a video, chances are you have a friend or two who might like that video, too. That's why YouTube lets you share the videos you like—in fact, this type of video sharing is a defining feature of the whole YouTube experience.

You share YouTube videos via email. That is, YouTube lets you send an email that contains a link to the video you like to your friends. When a friend receives this email, he or she can click the link in the message to go to YouTube and play the video.

Sharing a Video via Email

When you want to share a video, go to that video's page and click the Share Video link in the box underneath the YouTube video player. This opens a new window, like the one shown in Figure 5.9. Enter the email addresses of the intended recipients (separate multiple addresses with commas), your name, and a personal message, if you want. Click the Send button, and in a few minutes your recipients will receive the message.

 You can also share videos from your Favorites list. Just click the Share Video button beneath the video you want to share; then proceed as normal.

Figure 5.9
Sharing a video via email.

The message your friends receive looks like the one shown in Figure 5.10. To view the video, all they have to do is click the video thumbnail. This opens a web browser, accesses the YouTube site, and starts playing the video you shared.

Figure 5.10
An email invitation to view a YouTube video.

Sharing a Playlist via Email

YouTube also lets you share complete playlists with your friends. Just go to your Playlists page, select a playlist, and then click the Share This Playlist link. You now see the familiar email window; fill in the necessary information, click the Send button, and the playlist invitation email is sent.

 You cannot share private playlists—only public ones.

Managing Your Friends and Contacts

Every time you share a video with a friend, that friend's email address gets added to your YouTube Friends & Contacts list. Then, the next time you send a sharing email, all the email addresses of your friends are displayed on the right side of the email window. Check those addresses to which you want to send the invitation; it's much easier than entering each address manually.

To manage the names in your YouTube Friends & Contacts list, click the My Account link at the top of any YouTube page. When the My Account page appears, scroll down to the Friends & Contacts section; then click the All Contacts link.

This displays the Friends & Contacts page, shown in Figure 5.11. All your contacts are displayed here. To remove a friend from this list, check the box next to that person's name and then click the Remove Contacts button. To add a person to a specific Friends or Family list, check that person's name and then select that list from the Copy Contacts To list. (You can create new lists by clicking the Create New List button.)

 To see whether a friend is already a YouTube member, enter that person's name in the See If Your Friends Are Already on YouTube box; then click the Search button. You can also invite your friends to become YouTube members; just click the Invite Your Friends to Join YouTube! link and follow the onscreen instructions.

Figure 5.11
Managing your YouTube Friends & Contacts.

6

Downloading YouTube Videos to Your PC— And Your iPod

Watching videos on YouTube is great, but it's annoying that you can't save those videos to your PC for later viewing when you're not connected to the YouTube site. Or can you?

Even though YouTube doesn't let you download its videos, other sites and software programs step in to get the job done. There are many options for downloading YouTube videos to your computer's hard drive—and even to your iPod, for portable viewing.

How to Save YouTube Videos to Your Hard Drive

YouTube is a streaming video service. That means that it streams its videos from its site to your computer screen; you don't actually download and save the videos to your computer.

However, several websites and software programs let you do what YouTube doesn't—save YouTube videos to your computer's hard drive. And after you've saved a YouTube video, you can watch it anytime you want, even if you're not connected to the Internet.

Downloading YouTube Videos with VideoDownloader

The easiest way to save your YouTube videos is to use a video downloader site designed just for that purpose. One such site is VideoDownloader (www.javimoya.com/blog/youtube_en.php), which works in conjunction with the FLV Player program to download and play your YouTube videos. (You can download the FLV Player program for free from the VideoDownloader site.)

 While VideoDownloader happens to be one of the most popular video downloader sites, most of these sites work in pretty much the same fashion.

To use VideoDownloader, start by going to the video you want to save in YouTube. In the information box on the YouTube video page, shown in Figure 6.1, is a URL for the video; highlight the URL with your mouse, right-click, and select Copy from the pop-up menu.

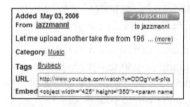

Figure 6.1
Copy the URL for the YouTube video from the information box.

Now go to the VideoDownloader page, shown in Figure 6.2. Position your cursor in the large box at the top of the page; then right-click your mouse and select Paste from the pop-up menu. This pastes the YouTube URL into the box.

Figure 6.2
Use VideoDownloader to download YouTube videos.

Next, pull down the Any Site list and select YouTube. (The Video-Downloader site downloads videos from a number of different video sharing sites.) Click the Download button, and VideoDownloader creates a download link for the video, as shown in Figure 6.3. Click the Download Link button, and when prompted click the Save button.

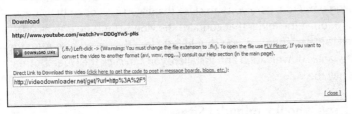

Figure 6.3
VideoDownloader creates a download link for the YouTube video.

Your computer now displays the Save As dialog box, shown in Figure 6.4. Here's where things get a little tricky. In addition to selecting a location to save the video file, you need to give the file a name and an extension. The name is up to you, but the file must have the .FLV extension. So, for example, if you want to save the file under the name **myvideo01**, you would enter **myvideo01.flv** into the File Name box. Click Save to save the file under its new name.

Info 4U .FLV is the file extension for Flash files. YouTube videos are stored and served as Flash files.

Figure 6.4
Saving the video as an FLV-format file.

When the download is complete, you see the Download Complete
dialog box. From here you can close the dialog box, open the video
file, or open the folder that contains the video. Until you download
the FLVPlayer software, you should just close the dialog box. After the
software is downloaded and installed, you can click the Open button
to play the video.

Other YouTube Downloader Sites

VideoDownloader is just one of several sites you can use to download YouTube videos. Similar downloader services are offered from
the following websites:

- dlThis.com Video Grabber (www.dlthis.com)
- FeelingTea (www.feelingtea.com/decode/google/)
- GooTube FLV Retriever (www.kej.tw/flvretriever/)
- KeepVid (www.keepvid.com)
- KissYouTube (www.kissyoutube.com)
- Ripzor YouTube Video Ripper
  (www.ripzor.com/youtuberipper.html)
- SaveTube (www.savetube.com)
- SaveYoutube.com (www.saveyoutube.com)

- TechCrunch YouTube Video Download Tool (www.techcrunch.com/get-youtube-movie/)
- VideoDL (www.videodl.org)
- YouTube Downloader (youtube.tdjc.be)
- YouTubeX.com (www.youtubex.com)
- YouTubia (www.youtubia.com)

Most of these sites work the same way as the VideoDownloader site. Copy the YouTube URL into the site, click a button, and then download the resulting file to your hard drive as an FLV-format file. You can then play the file with the FLVPlayer program.

 If you use the Internet Explorer web browser, you can use the FlvGetter plug-in (www.exploseek.com/FlvGetter/) to download FLV-format videos from within the browser. If you use Mozilla Firefox instead, similar FLV downloading plug-ins for your browser include UnPlug (addons.mozilla.org/firefox/2254/) and VideoDownloader (addons.mozilla.org/firefox/2390/).

Playing YouTube Videos with FLV Player

As you recall, YouTube videos are all served in the Flash FLV file format. When you save a YouTube video from a video downloader site, you're saving the video in an FLV-format file.

To play the FLV-format videos you download, you need a video player program for that format. Unfortunately, neither Windows Media Player nor the iTunes software can play back FLV-format files. That's why you want to download the FLV Player program (www.applian.com/flvplayer/). Fortunately, the program is free.

Other popular FLV players include

- Flash Guru Flash Video Player (free, www.flashguru.co.uk/free-tool-flash-video-player/)
- Flash Video Player (free, www.jeroenwijering.com/?item=Flash_Video_Player)
- Riva FLV Player (free, www.rivavx.com)

■ Wimpy Standalone FLV Player (free, www.wimpyplayer.com/products/wimpy_standalone_flv_player.html).

Figure 6.5 shows the FLV Player program in action. It launches automatically if you click Open in the Download Complete dialog box; otherwise, you can open it from within Windows or your Mac, and then click the File button to select a file to play.

Figure 6.5
Viewing a YouTube video in FLV Player.

Underneath the main video window in the FLV Player are the player's transport controls. In left-to-right order, you have Play/Pause, Stop, Rewind, and Forward. (For some reason, the Stop, Rewind, and Forward buttons all return the player to the beginning of the current video.) Next to these controls are the elapsed time display, the Mute button, and the volume control.

 The only drawback to using the FLV Player is that you're limited to viewing the video at its original size. FLV Player offers no full-screen option.

How to Convert YouTube Videos to Other File Formats

YouTube videos are all in Flash (FLV) format, which is why you need an FLV player to play them after you've downloaded them to your hard disk. Another option, however, is to convert those Flash format videos to another format that other video player programs (such as Windows Media Player or the iTunes player) can play.

File Conversion Programs

To convert an FLV-format file to another format, you need a video file conversion program. Many of these programs are available, and they all let you convert files to AVI, MPEG, WMV, and similar formats that most video player programs can handle.

The most popular of these file conversion programs include

- Moyea FLV to Video Converter ($39.95, www.flash-video-mx.com/flv_to_video_web/)
- Replay Converter ($29.95, www.applian.com/replay-converter/)
- Riva FLV Encoder (free, www.rivavx.com)
- Total Video Converter ($45.95, www.effectmatrix.com/total-video-converter/)
- Xilisoft FLV Converter ($29, www.xilisoft.com/flv-converter.html)

These programs all work similarly. You identify the FLV file you want to convert, specify an output file format, and then click the Convert button. A copy of the original file is created in the new file format you specified.

File Converting Online

One website performs both the downloading and the file conversion process, no software required. The vixy.net Online FLV Converter (www.vixy.net), shown in Figure 6.6, lets you input the YouTube video URL and choose a file output format. It then downloads and converts the YouTube file to the format you specified. This site converts files to the following formats: AVI, MOV, MP4 (ideal for iPod use), and 3GP (for video-enabled mobile phones).

Figure 6.6
Downloading and converting YouTube files with the Online FLV Converter.

How to Transfer YouTube Videos to Your iPod

If you have a fifth-generation video iPod, you're always looking for new (and low-cost) videos to play on your iPod. YouTube videos are ideal for iPod playback—after they've been properly converted, that is.

YouTube-to-iPod Converter Programs

Several programs available convert downloaded FLV-format YouTube videos to the MPEG-4 file format (with .MP4 or .MPV file extensions) used by the iPod. The most popular Windows-compatible programs include these:

- Free YouTube to iPod Converter (free, www.dvdvideosoft.com)
- iTube (free, www.benjaminstrahs.com/itube.php)
- Ivy Video Converter ($15, www.ipodsoft.com)

In addition, many of the converter programs listed in the previous section also output to an iPod-friendly video format. And if you want a YouTube conversion program that works on Macintosh computers, TubeSock ($15, www.stinkbot.com/Tubesock/) is the software to get.

 Online, the vixy.net Online FLV Converter (www.vixy.net) downloads and converts any YouTube video to iPod video format, no software necessary. The service is free.

Downloading and Converting with iTube

My favorite iPod converter is iTube, a free program that offers some nice features, chief among them the ability to perform both the download and the conversion process in a single step. (That is, you don't have to download the videos first, outside the program.) When you launch iTube, you see the dialog box shown in Figure 6.7. Enter the YouTube video URL into the Page URL box; then click Go. iTube downloads the video, automatically converts it to iPod format, and then imports it into your iTunes video library. The next time you connect your iPod to your computer, the video is transferred to your iPod for viewing on the go. It's the easiest way I know to download YouTube videos to your iPod.

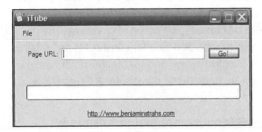

Figure 6.7
iTube downloads and converts YouTube videos to iPod format.

Downloading YouTube Videos—Is It Legal?

Some people question whether downloading and saving a YouTube video to your hard disk is legal. Although I'm not a lawyer, my opinion is an unequivocal "yes." All you're doing is watching a YouTube video in a slightly different fashion; instead of watching a streaming version of the video in your web browser, you're watching a stored version of the video from your hard disk. No harm, no foul.

It might be different, however, if you used that downloaded video for some purpose other than your own private viewing. YouTube's terms of use prohibit unauthorized use of users' videos, stating that:

> *Content on the website is provided to you AS IS for your information and personal use only and may not be used, copied, reproduced, distributed, transmitted, broadcast, displayed, sold,*

licensed, or otherwise exploited for any other purposes whatsoever without the prior written consent of the respective owners.

So if you download a video and then copy that file to your website or sell a DVD containing that video, you're violating YouTube's terms of use. What you're doing may or may not be legal, but you're breaking the terms you agreed to when you signed up for the YouTube service.

YouTube has (sporadically) taken a hardline interpretation of this particular clause, specifically in regard to the third-party download sites discussed earlier in this chapter. In November 2006, YouTube issued a cease and desist order to TechCrunch, which operates its own Video Download Tool for YouTube videos (www.techcrunch.com/get-youtube-movie/). YouTube claims that since the TechCrunch tool makes unauthorized copies of YouTube videos on its own servers, it is violating the "may not be copied" part of the terms of use. The letter also alleged that TechCrunch's downloader constitutes an "unfair business practice" under California law, and that TechCrunch's unauthorized use of the YouTube trade name constitutes a type of false advertising.

While TechCrunch has yet to buckle in to YouTube's demands, and YouTube has not filed formal legal action, it is interesting that YouTube is focusing on the copy-versus-stream distinction. In a follow-up letter sent to the TechCrunch site, YouTube's attorney drew attention to the fact that YouTube is a streaming-only service and that the company's terms of use do not permit users to download the videos hosted on the site. Here's a subsequent letter sent from YouTube's general counsel to the TechCrunch site:

Currently, YouTube is a streaming-only service. We do not permit users to download the videos we host on our site. We believe our Terms of Use are clear on this point, but in light of the confusion which came to our attention today we are considering revisions to our Terms of Use to avoid any further confusion. It is important to many of our users who have uploaded and licensed content to YouTube that their content is authorized for streaming-only.

It seems that YouTube is more concerned with copyright violations of its users' content than it is with prohibiting downloads per se. That is, YouTube doesn't want its content providers to sue YouTube because people downloaded their videos, instead of watching them streamed from YouTube's servers.

If YouTube wants to push the matter, downloading and saving YouTube videos could be prohibited—and the various third-party downloader sites could be shut down. Until that happens, however, I'd say that you're free to download to your heart's content, just as long as you're downloading for your own private use only.

YouTube 4 Video Makers

7

What Type of Videos Do *You* Want to Upload?

So far you've learned how to view various types of videos on YouTube. But YouTube is about more than just watching videos; it's also about sharing videos that you upload.

What kinds of videos can you upload to YouTube? For a Standard user, the only limitations are technical and content-related—videos can be no longer than 10 minutes or no larger than 100MB, can't contain adult or offensive content, and can't violate any copyrights. Past those parameters, anything you choose to upload is fair game. It's all a matter of what interests you—and what interests other YouTube users.

What Type of YouTuber Are You?

When it comes to uploading and sharing videos on YouTube, everyone has different tastes. Some people like to upload their home movies, others like to upload TV clips they've recorded, still others like to use YouTube for their personal video blogs or to promote their businesses. It all comes down to the question: What type of YouTuber are you?

The Recorder/Sharer

Lots and lots and lots of videos on YouTube are clips from recorded television shows. We're talking funny clips from *Saturday Night Live*, outrageous clips from *The View* and *Oprah*, entertaining clips from the latest concert or awards show, important clips from the nightly news—you name it.

YouTube is a great place to share all these different types of recorded clips. When you watch something you think others might find interesting, make sure you record it and then you can upload it to YouTube to share with the world.

To do this, the best approach is to record your TV programs digitally, either on your computer (if your PC contains a TV tuner) or with a digital video recorder (DVR), such as a TiVo or similar device. If you use a DVR, you'll need to somehow transfer your videos to your computer, where you'll use video editing software to edit the larger recording down to a shorter clip that you can upload. Naturally, you'll also use your computer to do the uploading to YouTube.

What kinds of TV clips are people interested in? Anything important, entertaining, or controversial is always good. That means key events, musical performances, funny routines or comments, rare appearances, even odd or humorous commercials; these types of clips get a lot of views on the YouTube site. (For example, Figure 7.1 shows just some of the clips on YouTube that document the alleged feud between *The View*'s Rosie O'Donnell and *The Apprentice*'s Donald Trump.)

Posting television clips has one major caveat, however. In almost all instances, anything you record off TV is copyrighted material. And, unless you happen to be the CEO of Viacom or NBC Universal, you probably don't own the copyright. So when you post a clip of a television show, you're infringing on the rights of the show's copyright owner.

The good news is many large media companies don't object to the posting of such clips; they view it (rightly, in this author's opinion) as free publicity for their programs. The bad news is other media companies object strenuously to this practice and will force YouTube to delete any clips of their shows from the site.

Figure 7.1
YouTube clips of the Rosie-Donald feud.

 One media company that doesn't like its clips on YouTube is Viacom. In February 2007, Viacom demanded that YouTube pull more than 100,000 unauthorized clips from Viacom programming—including *The Daily Show*, *The Colbert Report*, and *South Park*. (Viacom subsequently sued YouTube for a cool $1 billion, alleging massive copyright infringement.) Other media companies, including NBC Universal and CBS, have less of a problem with this practice and actually sponsor their own official YouTube channels.

So should you post television recordings on YouTube? That's up to you; you definitely risk having your clips pulled if you record the wrong shows from the wrong companies. But there's a big audience out there for relevant and entertaining TV clips—big enough that you'll probably have to work fast to be the first to post any given clip.

The Historian/Enthusiast

Posting clips from current TV shows is one thing; posting clips from older programming is something else. When it comes to uploading classic television programs and commercials, we're talking material of historical interest. And there's a lot of that type of historical video on YouTube.

Take, for example, the topic of vintage toy commercials—that is, the original commercials for what are now regarded as vintage toys. Search YouTube for "toy commercial" and get results such as those shown in Figure 7.2—commercials from the 1950s, 1960s, and 1970s for toys such as Johnny Reb, G.I. Joe, Hot Wheels, Mego superheroes action figures, and the like. Whether you're a television historian, a toy collector, or just a baby boomer nostalgic for his youth, these commercials are fascinating—and big draws on the YouTube site.

Figure 7.2
Vintage toy commercials on YouTube.

The same thing with classic musical performances. In the pre-MTV age, musicians performed (or lip synced) on shows like *Hullaballoo*, *Shindig*, and *The Ed Sullivan Show*. Some of those performances were taped, kinescoped, or otherwise recorded, and have made their way to YouTube. (For example, Figure 7.3 shows a selection of clips from the old *Hullaballoo* show.)

If you happen to own some of these classic clips, I guarantee that thousands of viewers would love to see them—and YouTube is the best way to get them seen. Classic TV show and commercial clips are some of the most popular categories of videos on YouTube; whether it's historical, nostalgic, or otherwise, the interest is definitely there.

Figure 7.3
Classic rock and roll performances from *Hullaballoo* on YouTube.

The Home Movie Maker

Of course, YouTube is more than just recorded television clips. A large percentage of the videos on YouTube are original, created by amateur movie makers with low-cost video cameras.

Why might you want to post your home movies on YouTube? Believe it or not, YouTube is a great place to share movies of your vacations, holidays, special events, and so on. Just upload your movies (no more than 10 minutes long apiece, of course), create a Group for your movies, and then invite your friends and family to that Group. They can access YouTube at their leisure and view all your home movies in their web browsers.

 Learn more about YouTube Groups in Chapter 12, "Joining the YouTube Community—And Creating Your Own Channel."

Sometimes your home movies can generate an audience well beyond friends and family. Think of the bloopers and funny moments in shows like *America's Funniest Home Videos* and then recognize that YouTube is the perfect place to share such videos with a much larger audience. Whether it's a short clip of you dancing (badly) to your favorite song, a video of your bride or groom falling face-down into the wedding cake, or a clip of you and your friends downhill sledding straight into a tree, if it's funny or memorable, YouTubers will embrace it. The more outrageous the clip, the more it will get passed along from user to user—and, in some instances, become viral. All you have to do is post the clip and let YouTube do the rest.

 A *viral video* is a video clip that gains widespread popularity via the Internet, typically via blog postings, email messages, and video sharing websites like YouTube.

And let's not forget cute animals. YouTube has a vast repository of video clips of cute kittens (such as those shown in Figure 7.4), puppies, ferrets, and the like. The cuter the animal the better—unless it's a really ferocious animal in a feeding frenzy. Stupid pet tricks are also good, as are dancing monkeys. So if you have a particularly videogenic pet around the house, get out your video camera and start making movie magic!

Figure 7.4
Everybody loves the cute kittens on YouTube.

The Video Blogger

YouTube is also a good place to distribute your own personal video blogs. A *video blog* (sometimes called a *vlog* or *video podcast*) is like a regular text-based blog, except that your personal comments are recorded on video. Typically, you sit in front of a video camera or webcam and start talking; it doesn't have to be fancy or have high production values. (Figure 7.5 shows a typical video blog from user boh3m3—just a guy and his webcam.) Post the resulting video to YouTube, and anyone on the site can watch your insightful musings. And, if viewers like your video blog, they can subscribe to your channel to view new uploads as you make them.

Figure 7.5
One of the more popular video blogs, from user boh3m3.

Info 4U Video bloggers are sometimes called *videographers*.

The Instructor

If you have information or instruction to impart to others, YouTube is the place to do it. That's right, YouTube is a great place to distribute short instructional videos—for free, of course.

Want to demonstrate how to build a bookcase? Or how to replace the power supply in a personal computer? Or shoot a perfect jump shot? Then grab your video camera, put together a quick how-to, and upload it to YouTube. (Figure 7.6 shows some of the many instructional videos available on YouTube.) You can direct interested parties to YouTube to view the video, or rely on people to stumble across it as they browse and search the YouTube site.

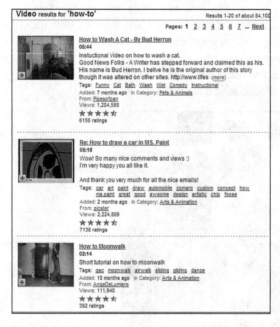

Figure 7.6
Instructional YouTube videos.

For that matter, if you're a professional educator, you can use YouTube to distribute classroom videos. Just make sure your lectures are less than 10 minutes long (or break longer ones into 10-minute segments) and then share the URLs with your students. Because hosting on YouTube is free, it's a great way to supplement your normal in-class instruction.

The Reporter

Everyone who has a digital camera (or a video camera built into a cell phone) is a potential news reporter. Amateur video makers can

capture all sorts of breaking events—a passing police chase, shoplift-
ing in process, a protest at city hall, wild weather conditions, you
name it. And when you capture something newsworthy, there's no
better place to share it than on YouTube. (Figure 7.7 shows a selection
of tornado videos uploaded by YouTube users.)

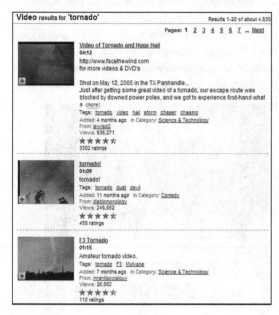

Figure 7.7
Amateur tornado videos on YouTube.

If your video is particularly newsworthy, it may be picked up by a professional news organization. More and more news shows—both local
and national—are using videos uploaded to YouTube to supplement
their internal reporting. This is especially so of breaking events that
are best captured on amateur video, the sort of thing that YouTube
does best.

The Performer

YouTube is a great place for musicians, comedians, and other per-
formers to distribute their wares. Thousands upon thousands of local
musicians upload their performance videos to YouTube for their fans

to view—or, hopefully, to be discovered by a major record label. And equal numbers of current and aspiring stand-up comedians tape their routines and post them to YouTube.

In fact, YouTube has created two distinct categories of membership just for these types of uploaders. Both the Musician and Comedian accounts let you augment your Channel page with your own custom background and logo, tour/show date information, and CD purchase links. (Figure 7.8 shows the Channel page for musician Ashley Tisdale.) You can use your YouTube videos to sell your CDs and other merchandise. This makes YouTube a nice home for yourself or your band.

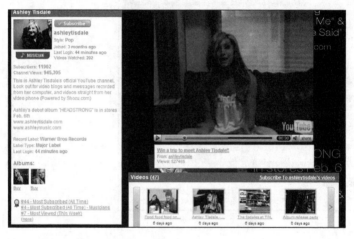

Figure 7.8
Ashley Tisdale's YouTube Musician Channel page—complete with links to purchase her CDs.

So if you're an up-and-coming performer, consider using YouTube as a promotional vehicle. Upload your performance videos, include your tour dates and CD purchase links, and make a direct connection with your fans.

The Aspiring Film Director

Of course, not all videos on YouTube are amateur videos. YouTube is also the home for many aspiring professional movie makers. (And for professional directors, as well; Figure 7.9 shows a short film from director Tim Burton.)

Figure 7.9
Tim Burton's 1983 short film, *The Flying Saucers and Me*—available for viewing on YouTube.

If you want to be a film director, YouTube is a great place to display your talents. YouTube makes it easy to upload any and all student films, independent films, and short videos that you've created. And, if you have a YouTube Director account, you can upload videos longer than the standard 10-minute limit—although you're still limited to the 100MB maximum file size.

 To apply for a Director account, go to www.youtube.com/premium_register.

After you've uploaded your films, you can direct potential clients or employers to YouTube to view them. You can also promote your films on YouTube; many shorts have become minor hits after being discovered by the YouTube user base. Put simply, YouTube is the premier venue for exposing all manner of amateur films to the viewing public—and to the major studios.

The Online Business

One more use of YouTube bears examination. Believe it or not, many businesses use YouTube to promote their products and companies by uploading commercials, promo spots, infomercials, and so on. It's a great way to build grassroots brand recognition—and attract new customers.

Examples of business-oriented videos include professional movie trailers, TV spots, long-form advertisements, internal communications videos, product support videos, and real estate video walk-throughs. (YouTube is going to be a big deal for realtors; Figure 7.10 shows some of the real estate videos available on YouTube.)

Figure 7.10
Real estate walk-throughs on the YouTube site.

When you post a video to YouTube, it takes on a life of its own. Your ad or infomercial will be viewed by thousands of YouTube users, posted to numerous websites and blogs, emailed around the Internet—you name it. Just make sure you tailor your message to the YouTube crowd, shoot the video with web playback in mind, and scale the video so that it looks best in the YouTube player. You should also point to the YouTube video in your other advertising, and even embed the video on your normal website.

What Makes a Great YouTube Video?

Whatever type of video you decide to upload to YouTube, you can do certain things to increase the number of viewers who watch it. Although there's no way to guarantee a large number of views, certain types of content tend to do better than others.

First, don't just upload any old video, and don't swamp the site with random uploads. Instead, develop some sort of a plan. Focus on a particular type of video, or a particular topic area. Targeting a small group of viewers is better than using a shotgun approach.

The best YouTube videos have something to say. They have a point of view, a personal voice, a reason to exist. Random images of cute kittens don't cut it, but a cute kitten snuggling up to a big, scary-looking dog tells a story of sorts. Inject intent and commentary into your videos, and they'll gain an audience.

Funny is also good. Let's face it, most folks go to YouTube to be entertained. So the funnier or more entertaining your video is, the more viewers it will attract.

Another way to attract viewers is to stand out from the crowd. The more unique your video is, the more attention it will draw to itself. I can't tell you how to be unique, but I can tell you not to do what everyone else does. The world of YouTube needs innovators, not imitators.

Here's something else to know. In general, short videos do better than longer ones. Don't bother with extended introductions and long codas; get right to the point and then get out. People don't like to waste a lot of time online, so keep your videos short and meaty—otherwise, users will click away before the videos are over.

In general, it pays to be professional. If you're shooting your own videos, use adequate lighting, set up attractive camera angles, and definitely make sure that your sound quality is up to snuff. Even amateur videos can look good—and better-looking videos attract more viewers than do dimly lit poor-sounding ones.

That said, play to the medium's strengths. Know that your video will be seen in a tiny window on a small computer screen and then shoot it accordingly. Use lots of close-ups, keep the background plain, avoid long shots, and employ simple images with high contrast. Visual sub-tlety is not your friend.

Along the same lines, don't skimp on the volume. A tinny computer speaker can only reproduce so much in terms of audio quality; keep the sound simple and the levels loud.

If you're posting a clip recorded from TV, use your video editing software to trim the clip to just its bare essentials. And don't be afraid to edit out dead or uninteresting bits in the middle, either. It's okay to edit.

It's not okay, however, to post something that dozens of other people have already posted. Search the site before you upload; YouTube doesn't need yet another clip of those cute kittens shown on the *Today* show last week. Avoid duplication; go for something unique.

You should also test your videos before you upload them. Just like the motion picture studios host test screenings of their films, you should show your videos to a few friends and family members before you post them to YouTube. Get your friends' honest reactions and then edit your videos in response. If nobody likes what they're see-ing, chances are the YouTube community won't either.

Finally, don't forget the tags. Most YouTube viewers find videos by searching, and the more targeted and appropriate your tags, the easier it will be for users to find your videos.

Warning 4U Because viewers can comment on all videos posted on YouTube, be prepared for at least a few negative comments. No matter how good you think your video is, someone somewhere is bound to disagree. If this bothers you, don't upload your videos!

8

Creating Videos 4 YouTube

You've decided what type of videos you want to share on YouTube. Now comes a technical decision—what's the best way to create those videos? YouTube, after all, accepts uploads in a limited number of file formats, and some of those formats probably work better than others. So what do you need to do to make the best YouTube-compatible videos?

Understanding YouTube File Formats

The first thing to know about creating videos for YouTube is which file format YouTube uses. For what it's worth, YouTube stores and serves its videos in the H.263 variant of the Adobe Flash video format, with a .FLV file extension. That said, you can't upload your videos in the Flash format; YouTube converts your videos to this format after they've been uploaded.

Instead, you upload your videos to YouTube in your choice of the MPEG-4 (.AVI or .MPG), QuickTime (.MOV), or Windows Media Video (.WMV) file formats. Once uploaded, YouTube automatically does the conversion to an FLV file.

But file format isn't the only important technical issue to keep in mind. Resolution and frame rate also affect the ultimate quality of your videos when they're played on YouTube. In particular, if you upload your videos at too high a resolution, YouTube will automatically downconvert them to 320×240 resolution—and, unfortunately, YouTube's downconversion often results in grainy or pixelated images. It's far better to create or convert videos yourself at the proper resolution.

So what are the best settings to use when creating or converting your videos? Here's the short list:

- MPEG-4 format video with either the DivX or XviD codecs
- MP3 format audio
- 320×240 resolution
- Frame rate of 30 frames per second (FPS)

Videos uploaded with these settings will look their best on the YouTube site.

 Unless you have a Director account, YouTube also requires that your videos be less than 10 minutes long and less than 100MB in file size.

Converting Existing Videos to YouTube Format

When creating a new video from scratch, it's easy enough to config- ure your recording device to use the settings just recommended. But what do you do if you want to upload an existing video that's in a dif- ferent format?

The task of converting videos from one format to another is the province of a video converter program. This type of software auto- matically does video file format conversion and in the process can also convert files from one resolution or size to another. If you have a lot of existing videos you want to upload to YouTube, you'll need one of these programs.

Some of the most popular video conversion programs include

- AVS Video Converter ($39.95, www.avsmedia.com/VideoTools/)
- M²Convert Professional ($89, www.m2solutionsinc.com/ m2convert-pro.htm)

- Movavi VideoSuite ($59.99, www.movavi.com/suite/)
- Power Video Converter ($29.95, www.apussoft.com)
- RER Video Converter ($23, www.rersoft.com/videoconverter.htm)
- VIDEOzilla ($29.95, www.videozilla.net)
- Xilisoft Video Converter ($35, www.xilisoft.com/video-converter.html), shown in Figure 8.1

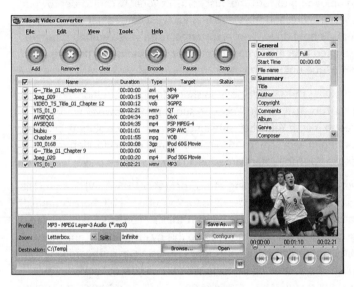

Figure 8.1
Use the Xilisoft Video Converter to convert existing videos to a YouTube-friendly format.

Using one of these converter programs is typically as easy as selecting the file to convert, choosing an output format, and then clicking the "convert" button. Other settings (such as resolution or frame rate) are sometimes available, but the basic conversion process is most often a one-click operation.

Shooting Videos for YouTube

Many YouTube videos are variations on the traditional home movie. That is, they're shot with consumer-grade video camcorders, and then edited and uploaded to the YouTube site.

The easiest way to shoot movies for YouTube is to use a digital video (DV) camcorder, which captures video digitally. The most popular type of digital camcorder uses the MiniDV tape format, although other digital camcorder formats will also do the job.

The reason you want to use a digital camcorder is that digital video can be easily transferred from your camcorder to your PC for editing and uploading to YouTube. Just connect your DV camcorder to your PC via FireWire, and the video files you've recorded get copied to your PC's hard drive. Once transferred, use a video editing program (discussed later in this chapter) to edit the videos and prepare them for YouTube uploading.

By the way, there's little point in shooting high-definition video (HDV) for YouTube use, as you'll need to substantially downconvert this video to match YouTube's substandard 320×240 resolution. Likewise, shooting in widescreen (16:9) mode merely results in a letterbox video in YouTube's standard aspect ratio (4:3) video player window.

If you have an older analog camcorder (VHS, VHS-C, SVHS, 8mm, Hi8, and the like), transferring videos for YouTube is a bit more complex. That's because you need to convert the camcorder's analog recordings to digital video format. You do this by installing an analog-to-digital video capture card in your PC, or using an outboard video capture device that connects to your PC via USB or FireWire. You'll plug your recorder into the jacks on the video capture card or device (typically using standard RCA connectors), and it will convert the analog signals from your recorder into the digital audio and video your computer understands.

Once converted to digital format, you can use a video editing program to edit and prepare the video for uploading to YouTube.

Capturing Webcam Video

If you plan on uploading videos for a video blog (vlog), the easiest approach might be to use a webcam to create your vlog entries. Although you could use a camcorder to do the job, that might be overkill—especially if your videos consist of you sitting at your desk and talking.

YouTube makes it easy to upload webcam videos. You can either save your webcam video to a standard video file, and then upload that file, or you can use YouTube's Quick Capture feature to upload a video as you record it, in real time. The latter method is quite easy to use, even if it doesn't allow you the luxury of editing the videos you record.

 Learn more about using Quick Capture to upload webcam videos in Chapter 9, "Uploading Videos to YouTube."

Capturing Television Programming

If you want to upload recorded television programming to YouTube, you first have to record that programming. The most efficient way to do this is with your PC, which means installing a TV tuner/capture card in your computer, or connecting an external USB TV tuner box. With such a card or box installed, your PC functions much like a television receiver, but with the added functionality of being able to record the television programs it receives. The recording is direct to your PC's hard disk in digital video format—perfect for editing and uploading to YouTube.

 Popular TV tuner cards are sold by AVerMedia (www.aver.com), Hauppauge (www.hauppauge.com), Pinnacle Systems (www.pinnaclesys.com), and similar companies. Prices are typically in the $100 range—or less.

If you have a TiVo or similar digital video recorder (DVR) connected to your living room television set, you may be able to use that device to capture video programming for YouTube use. Obviously, you're already recording shows with this device; recording is digital to the unit's built-in hard disk. The challenge, however, is transferring the recorded video from that unit to your PC so that you can edit the video and upload the recording to YouTube.

Most cable and satellite company DVRs have limited output options. For example, the Scientific American box provided by my cable company only lets me output analog audio and video. If I want to transfer a recording from my DVR to my PC, I have to connect analog audio and video cables between my DVR and an analog-to-digital video capture card or box connected to my PC and then play back the recording on the DVR. My PC then captures the analog output from my DVR and converts it to digital format—in real time. Not only is it a kludgy solution, the resulting video quality is subpar.

If you have a TiVo DVR, you can use the TiVo Desktop software (www.tivo.com/desktop/) to do the job for you. This free software automatically transfers recordings from your TiVo unit to your PC in digital format. It's almost as easy as recording directly on your PC.

Warning 4U TiVo frowns on the uploading of recorded content and embeds a watermark in all the recordings you make that link a recording to a specific TiVo user account. If a copyright holder wants to identify and prosecute someone who's illegally uploaded a copy of their content, they can use the embedded TiVo copyright to track you down.

Ripping Video from DVDs

Not that it's recommended (there are probably copyright issues), but you can copy video from DVDs to your PC and then upload those videos to YouTube. Assuming that you're not ripping an encoded movie DVD, plenty of software solutions are available that let you perform this task.

Info 4U The process of copying audio and video from a DVD or CD to a PC's hard disk is called *ripping*.

Some of the more popular DVD rippers include

- #1 DVD Ripper ($34.95, www.dvdtox.com)
- 321Soft DVD Ripper ($29.95, www.321soft.com/dvd-ripper.html)
- dvdXsoft DVD Ripper ($35, www.dvdxsoft.com/dvd-ripper.html), shown in Figure 8.2
- InterVideo WinDVD ($59.95, www.intervideo.com/WinDVD/)
- Magic DVD Ripper ($35, www.magicdvdripper.com)
- Xilisoft DVD Ripper ($35, www.xilisoft.com/dvd-ripper.html)

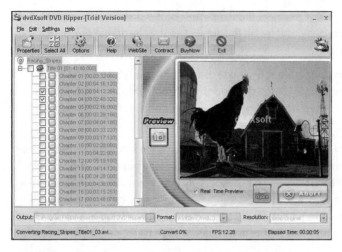

Figure 8.2
Use the dvdXsoft DVD Ripper to copy DVD content to your hard disk—and then to YouTube.

Once ripped (presumably in MPEG-4 format), you can edit the video to a YouTube-friendly, less-than-10-minute-length and then upload the resulting video to YouTube.

Shooting Great YouTube Videos

When shooting a video for YouTube, it's important to get the file format and technical details right. It's also important to get the visual details right—to create a video that is visually and stylistically interesting to YouTube viewers.

Whether you're shooting with an expensive digital camcorder or a cheap computer webcam, the most important thing to remember is that people will view your video in a small window in their web browser. You must create a video that looks good at this small size, viewed on a typical computer screen.

What does this mean in terms of visual style? Big and bright is the order of the day. You can shoot an epic with a cast of thousands, but those thousands will look like little dots at YouTube's default 320x240 resolution. The best YouTube videos are visually simple, with a single main subject filling up most of the small video window. Get up close, and frame the subject so that he or it fills most of the screen.

When using a webcam, that means getting up close to the lens. When using a camcorder, you should zoom into the main subject, and remove any unnecessary people or objects from the frame. Close-ups are good; crowd shots aren't.

You also want to make sure the scene you're shooting is adequately lit. Too many YouTube videos come out way too dark, which makes them hard to view. This is especially important when you're shooting with a webcam; even though a webcam might claim to work under normal room light, you're better served by investing in a set of afford-able photo floodlights or a separate speed light.

Finally, know that streaming video doesn't always reproduce rapid movement well. Move the camera too fast—or have your subject move too fast in the frame—and viewers are likely to see motion smears, pixilation, and other unacceptable video effects. Keep things slow and simple for best results.

Editing Videos Before You Upload

Few videos are YouTube-ready out of the box. No, you'll probably want to cut out the boring parts, trim the whole thing down to no more than 10 minutes (less is probably better), and convert the video to a YouTube-friendly 320×240 MPEG-4 file.

How do you do all this? With a video editing program, of course.

Video editing software performs many of the same functions as the professional editing consoles you might find at your local television station. You can use video editing software to cut entire scenes from your video, rearrange scenes, add fancy transitions between scenes, add titles (and subtitles), and even add your own music soundtrack. The results are amazing!

If you have a Windows PC, the most popular video editing programs include

■ Adobe Premiere Elements ($99.99, www.adobe.com/products/premiereel/)

- Adobe Premiere Pro ($849, www.adobe.com/products/premiere/)
- Pinnacle Studio ($69.99, www.pinnaclesys.com)
- Ulead MediaStudio Pro ($399.99, www.ulead.com/msp/)

In addition, both Windows XP and Windows Vista include a full-featured video editing program—and it's free! The program is called Windows Movie Maker, and although it's not as sophisticated as some of the other video editing programs, it should include all the features you need to do basic home video editing. Figure 8.3 shows the Windows Vista version of Windows Movie Maker in action.

Figure 8.3
Use Windows Movie Maker to edit your movies for YouTube use.

If you're a Macintosh user, you have Apple's iMovie software already installed. Like Windows Movie Maker, iMovie is a surprisingly full-featured video editing program, and it's also free.

Remember, save your final video in an .AVI or .MPG file, at 320×240 resolution (if you have that choice). It's better to do this conversion in the video editing program than to let YouTube do it; the results are noticeably superior.

 Videos all converted and edited? Learn how to upload your videos in Chapter 9, "Uploading Videos to YouTube."

9

Uploading Videos to YouTube

Okay. You've decided what type of video you want to create. You've made the video and converted it to the proper format. Now it's time to take the final step and upload the video to YouTube.

Read on to learn how.

Uploading Videos from Your Computer

Most YouTubers upload videos that are stored on their PC's hard disk. YouTube makes this kind of PC-based upload extremely easy.

Assuming that your video is in a YouTube-approved format, is less than 10 minutes long, and the file is smaller than 100MB, you're ready to upload. You start by clicking the Upload Videos link in the top right-hand corner of any YouTube page. This displays the Video Upload page shown in Figure 9.1. You now have a little paperwork to do.

Video Upload (Step 1 of 2)
All fields are required

Uploading a video is a two-step process—on the next page, you'll be able to choose your video file and set the privacy settings. Uploads will usually take 1-5 minutes per MB on a high-speed connection, and converting your video takes a few minutes; you can add more info or upload more videos while it's processing.

Unless you have been pre-approved for longer videos, your video is limited to 10 minutes and 100MB. For more details about uploading videos, see the Help Center.

Title:

Description:

Tags:

Enter one or more tags, separated by spaces.
Tags are keywords used to describe your video as it can be easily found by other users. For example, if you have a surfing video, you might tag it surfing beach waves

Video Category:
○ Autos & Vehicles ○ Comedy ○ Entertainment
○ Film & Animation ○ Gadgets & Games ○ Howto & DIY
○ Music ○ News & Politics ○ People & Blogs
○ Pets & Animals ○ Sports ○ Travel & Places

Language: English

Copyright Notice
Do not upload copyrighted material for which you don't own the rights or have permission from the owner.

Continue Uploading Or Use Quick Capture

Figure 9.1
Getting ready to upload your video to YouTube.

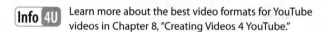 **Info 4U** Learn more about the best video formats for YouTube videos in Chapter 8, "Creating Videos 4 YouTube."

First enter a title for your video. Make sure it's descriptive without being overly long. Next enter a description for the video; this can (and should) be longer and more complete.

Then enter one or more tags for the video, separating each tag by a space. Tags are keywords people use when searching; use as many tags as necessary to capture all possible search words.

Now scroll down and select a category for the video, as well as the language that the video is in. Click the Continue Uploading button when you're ready to proceed.

Step two of the video upload process, shown in Figure 9.2, is where you specify the file to upload. Click the Browse button to open the

Select File to Upload dialog box, shown in Figure 9.3. Navigate to and
select the file you want and then click Open. This loads the filename
into the File box on the Video Upload page.

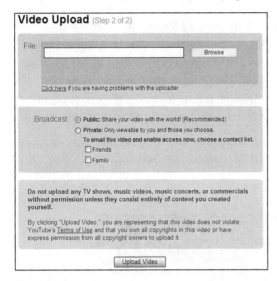

Figure 9.2
Step two of the video upload process.

Figure 9.3
Selecting a video to upload.

Next, select whether you want the video to be public or private. A
public video can be viewed by any YouTube user; a private video can
be viewed only by selected friends and family.

Use the private option when you're sharing home videos with friends and family, or if you have a real estate walk-through to show to selected clients.

All that done, the final step is to click the Upload Video button. YouTube finds the video on your hard disk and starts uploading it; the progress is shown on the Video Upload page.

After the video is uploaded, YouTube displays the Edit My Videos page. This is where you can fine-tune the listing for your video. In particular, you'll want to make the following edits, as appropriate:

▧ In the Video Details section, shown in Figure 9.4, make any necessary changes to the title, description, and tags.

Figure 9.4
Editing video details.

▧ In the Date & Location Details section, shown in Figure 9.5, enter the date the video was recorded and where it was recorded (location, country, and Zip code).

In the Sharing section, shown in Figure 9.6, note the URL for the video, as well as the HTML to be used for embedding the video, and then check whether the video is public or private; whether you want the link to the video emailed to people on your Friends or Family lists; whether you want to allow comments (with or without your approval); whether you want to allow video responses (with or without your approval); whether you want to let viewers rate your video; and whether you want to allow external sites to embed your video.

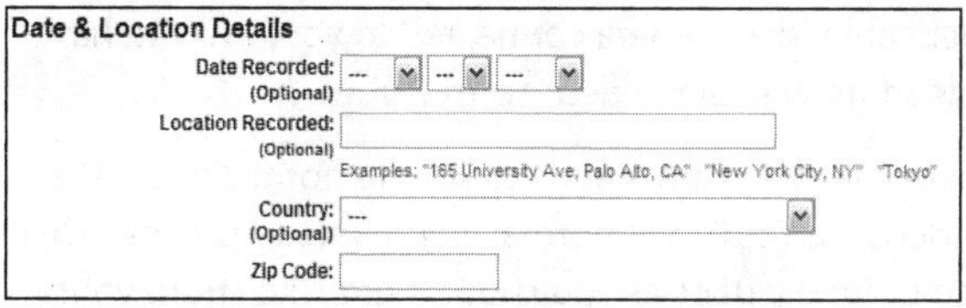

Figure 9.5
Entering date and location details.

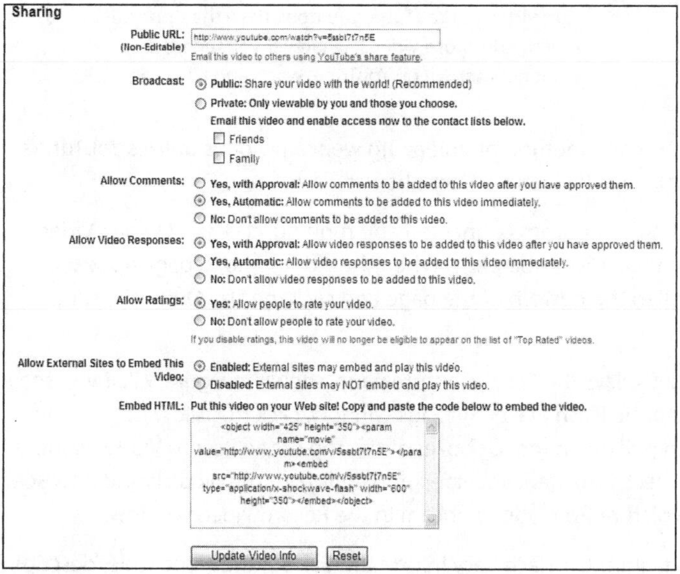

Figure 9.6
Selecting video sharing options.

Click the Update Video Info button when you're finished editing.

To view your video, click the My Videos link on any YouTube page and then click the thumbnail for your new video. Note that videos you uploaded are not immediately available for viewing on YouTube; they must first be processed and approved by the site, which can take anywhere from a few minutes to a few hours.

Uploading Videos from Your Webcam

If you have a webcam video camera connected to your PC, you have two ways of uploading webcam videos to YouTube.

First, you can save your webcam videos as you do normally and then upload those videos via YouTube's normal video upload process. Or, if you like, you can upload videos as you shoot them, "live" from your webcam.

 When you use Quick Capture to upload "live" webcam videos to YouTube, you don't have the opportunity to edit those videos; whatever you record is what gets shown on YouTube, warts and all.

This second method of uploading webcam videos utilizes YouTube's Quick Capture feature. Here's how it works.

With your webcam connected and running, click the Upload Videos link on any YouTube page. When the Video Upload page appears, scroll to the bottom of the page and click the Use Quick Capture button.

This displays the Quick Capture page, shown in Figure 9.7. If you see an Adobe Flash Player Settings window, click the Allow button and then pull down the list boxes at the top of the Record Video window to select your webcam video and audio options; you should now see the picture from your webcam in the Record Video window.

Next, enter the necessary information about the video (title, description, tags, category, and language) and then click the Record button to start your recording. When you're finished with the recording, click the Done button.

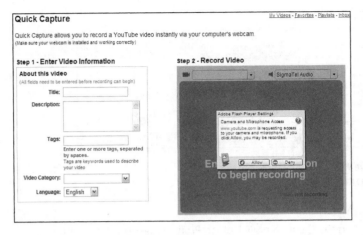

Figure 9.7
Recording a "live" webcam video with Quick Capture.

YouTube automatically uploads the video to the site and displays the Edit Information page. Enter or edit information as necessary, and let YouTube process the video for viewing.

 If you don't like what you just recorded, click the Re-Record button for a do-over.

Uploading Videos from Your Mobile Phone

Finally, if your mobile phone has a built-in video camera, you can upload videos directly from your cell phone without first copying them to your PC. All you have to do is set up YouTube's mobile upload options and then email your videos to the YouTube site.

To configure YouTube for your mobile phone, click the My Account link at the top of any YouTube page. When your My Account page appears, scroll down to the Account Settings section and click the Mobile Upload Profiles link. When the next page appears, as shown in Figure 9.8, click the Create Mobile Profile button.

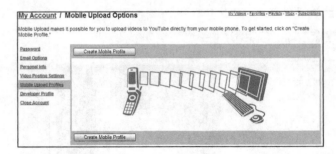

Figure 9.8
Getting ready to create a new mobile upload profile.

When the Create Mobile Upload Profile page appears, as shown in Figure 9.9, supply the necessary information—the profile name, video title, whether you want the filename or date appended to the video title, a short description of the profile, whether your mobile videos should be public or private, tags for your mobile videos, a category for your videos, whom you want to share them with, and how you want to be notified when the upload is complete. Click the Create Profile button, and your profile is created.

Figure 9.9
Creating a profile for uploading mobile videos.

As you can see in Figure 9.10, your profile includes the email address to which you should send your mobile videos, typically a series of numbers @mms.youtube.com. Note this address and enter it into your mobile phone's address book.

To upload a video from your mobile phone, simply email the video to this address. You'll be notified via email or text message when YouTube has received the email and begun processing the video; you can then go to YouTube's website and edit specific information about the newly uploaded video.

Figure 9.10
Your new mobile upload video—email your mobile phone videos to the email address listed here.

10

Managing Your Uploaded Videos

In the previous chapter you learned how to upload videos to YouTube. Your work's not done, however; you still have to manage your videos, block unwanted viewers, view user comments and ratings, and so on.

Editing Video Information

As discussed in Chapter 9, "Uploading Videos to YouTube," you can edit any and all information entered about your video on the Edit My Videos page. You get to this page by clicking the My Videos link on the YouTube home page; this displays a list of all the videos you've uploaded, as shown in Figure 10.1. From here, click the Edit Video Info button underneath the video you want to edit.

The fun begins when the Edit My Videos page appears, as shown in Figure 10.2. Here you can edit the video's title, description, tags, category, language, date and location details, sharing details, and the like. Click the Update Video info button when you're done editing.

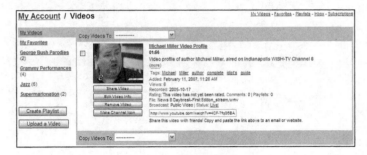

Figure 10.1
Click the Edit Video Info button to edit information for a specific video.

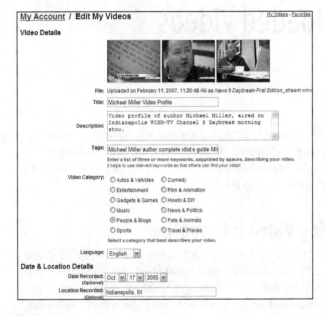

Figure 10.2
Editing video information.

 What can you do if you don't like the thumbnail image that YouTube chooses for your video? Nothing, unfortunately. YouTube doesn't have a facility to choose your own thumbnail image, so you have to live with the image that YouTube automatically selects.

Removing a Video from YouTube

When a video has run its course you can remove it from the YouTube site; otherwise, it'll stay online forever. (Or until YouTube goes out of business, whichever comes first.) To remove a video from YouTube, click the My Videos link on the YouTube home page to display the list of all your videos; click the Remove Video button below the video you want to delete. It's that simple.

 Think twice before you click the Remove Video button. All videos you remove are permanently deleted from the YouTube site. You'll need to re-upload the video if you click the Remove Video button by mistake.

Dealing with Viewers and Viewer Comments

One of the fun things about uploading videos to YouTube is that you get to see the comments and responses from people who've viewed your videos. Although this can be fun, it isn't always pleasant—which is why YouTube lets you manage these comments.

Enabling or Disabling Comments and Video Responses

Viewers can leave both text comments and video responses to your videos—if you let them. At your discretion, you can allow, disallow, or allow with prior approval either comments or video responses for any individual video you upload. (This means you can allow comments for one video while disallowing comments for another.)

To control comments and video responses, click the My Videos link on the YouTube home page to display the list of all your videos; click the Edit Video Info button below the video you want to control.

When the Edit My Videos page appears, scroll down to the Sharing section. In particular, you're interested in the Allow Comments and Allow Video Responses options, shown in Figure 10.3. For either option you can choose the following settings:

- **Yes, with Approval**—Viewers can submit comments and video responses, but you have to approve these comments/responses before they appear on your video page.

Allow Comments:	○ Yes, with Approval: Allow comments to be added to this video after you have approved them.
	⊙ Yes, Automatic: Allow comments to be added to this video immediately.
	○ No: Don't allow comments to be added to this video.
Allow Video Responses:	⊙ Yes, with Approval: Allow video responses to be added to this video after you have approved them.
	○ Yes, Automatic: Allow video responses to be added to this video immediately.
	○ No: Don't allow video responses to be added to this video.

Figure 10.3
Enabling or disabling comments and video responses.

■ **Yes, Automatic**—Viewers can submit comments and video responses, and these comments/responses appear immediately on your video page.

■ **No**—The comments and video responses sections do not appear on your video page.

Make sure you click the Update Video Info button after you've made any changes to these options.

Approving Comments and Video Responses

If you choose the "With Approval" option for comments or video responses, you have to manually approve any comments or responses viewers post to this video. When a viewer posts a comment or response, YouTube sends you an email, like the one in Figure 10.4. Thus notified, go to the YouTube site and click the email link at the top of any YouTube page, and then click the Video Comments (for text comments) or Video Responses (for video responses) link.

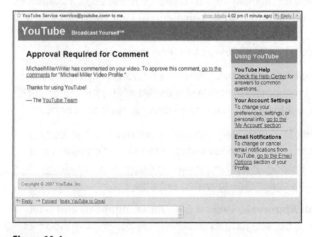

Figure 10.4
YouTube sends an email notification when you receive a comment or response to your video.

As you can see in Figure 10.5, this displays a list of all pending comments/responses in your inbox. Click the message link to display the comment, as shown in Figure 10.6. From here you can choose from the following options:

Figure 10.5
Pending comments and responses in your YouTube inbox.

Figure 10.6
Responding to a viewer comment.

- **Reply**—Click to post a reply to a viewer comment.
- **Remove**—Click to disallow a pending comment, or remove a previously approved comment.
- **Block User**—Click to block a user from posting future comments.
- **Approve**—Click to approve and post this specific comment to your video page.
- **Spam**—Click to report this comment to YouTube as spam.

So to approve a comment or response to your video, click the Approve link. To not approve a comment, click the Remove link.

Removing Viewer Comments and Responses

As you just learned, you can remove viewer comments and responses from the Video Comments and Video Responses sections of your YouTube inbox. You can also remove comments from the video page itself. Make sure you're signed in to YouTube; then go to the video page. Find the comment or video response you want to remove and then click the Remove link beneath that comment/response, as shown in Figure 10.7. Easy!

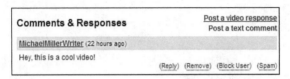

Figure 10.7
Removing an unwanted comment—click the Remove link.

Blocking Members from Leaving Comments

Every now and then you'll run into a virtual stalker; some disgruntled type who delights in leaving negative comments on all your videos. Although you can manually remove all of this user's comments, a better approach is to keep him from leaving those comments in the first place.

To this end, YouTube lets you block members from leaving comments and responses (and from sending personal messages to your YouTube inbox). To block a user, all you have to do is click on that member's name to access his channel/profile page, scroll to the Connect With box (shown in Figure 10.8), and click the Block User link. This user will now be blocked from commenting on your videos and contacting you.

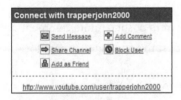

Figure 10.8
Block a user from his or her channel/profile page.

You can also block a user who's commented on your video, directly from the video page. Just click the Block User link under that user's comments.

Unsubscribing Users from Your Channel

In addition to blocking user comments, you may also want to get rid of unwelcome subscribers to your video channel. You do this by clicking the My Account link at the top of any YouTube page; when the My Account page appears, scroll down to the Subscriptions & Subscribers section and click the Subscribers to My Videos link. This displays a list of members subscribed to your videos, as shown in Figure 10.9. To remove a subscriber, simply click the Unsubscribe link under the subscriber's name.

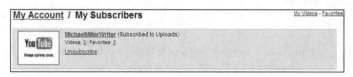

Figure 10.9
Removing a subscriber to your video channel.

 Learn more about channels in Chapter 12, "Joining the YouTube Community—And Creating Your Own Channel."

Viewing and Managing Video Ratings

The other way that users can provide feedback on your videos is via YouTube's rating system. As you recall, videos can be rated on a scale of 1 to 5 stars, with 5 stars being the best and 1 star being the worst.

You can't rate your own videos, of course, but you can view the average rating of the other users who've viewed your videos. Just go to the video page and scroll to the options box below the video player; the current star rating will be displayed there.

You also have the option of not allowing viewers to rate your video. This may be desirable if you have private home movies posted, or real estate walk-throughs, or other types of videos that you don't want to be perceived in a negative fashion.

To turn off ratings for a specific video, click the My Videos link on YouTube's home page and then click the Edit Video Info button beneath that video. When the Edit My Videos page appears, scroll down to the Sharing section and the Allow Ratings option, shown in Figure 10.10. The default setting is Yes; select No if you don't want viewers to rate this video. Click the Update Video Info button when finished.

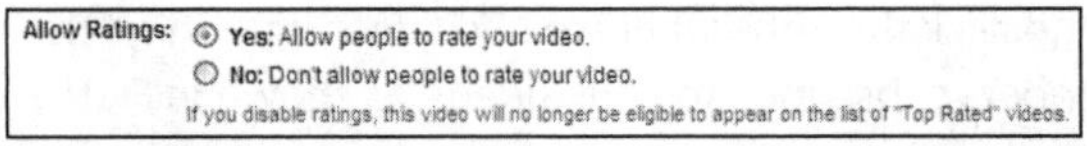

Allow Ratings:	⊙ **Yes:** Allow people to rate your video.
	○ **No:** Don't allow people to rate your video.
	If you disable ratings, this video will no longer be eligible to appear on the list of "Top Rated" videos.

Figure 10.10
Disabling ratings for a video.

Want to increase your YouTube ratings? Then check out the tips in Chapter 14, "Profiting from Your YouTube Videos."

Who Owns What: Legal Issues with YouTube Videos

YouTube is a video sharing site, to which users can upload virtually any type of video. As you can imagine, this causes more than a few problems, as some users are apt to upload videos that aren't their own—that is, copyrighted videos copied from another source. And sometimes that other source objects to their videos being shared on YouTube in this fashion. When this happens, problems ensue.

Dealing with Copyright Infringement Issues

Here's the deal. You can upload just about any video to YouTube—everything from amateur home movies to clips you've recorded from TV to movies you've ripped from commercial DVDs. But just because you can upload the video doesn't mean that you have the right to do so. And if you upload something you shouldn't, YouTube will pull it from the site.

The Legal Issue

One of YouTube's biggest challenges is managing the issue of copyright infringement. Users post illegally copied videos to the site, the copyright owners find out about it and complain to YouTube, and then YouTube pulls those infringing videos.

This puts YouTube in an awkward position, both operationally and legally. Operationally, it has to spend considerable amounts of resources to respond to these complaints, evaluate questionable videos, and then pull the videos from the site. Legally, YouTube quite possibly is leaving itself open to the same type of industry legal action that closed down numerous audio file sharing sites, such as the original Napster.

That said, YouTube seems to go out of its way to accommodate the demands of copyright holders. It responds quickly to complaints and has a track record of pulling offending videos and kicking serial offenders off the site. (This does not always endear YouTube to its user base, of course.) In addition, YouTube is working closely with big media companies to obtain formal licenses for broad swaths of content, to the point of creating company-specific channels for major networks, music labels, and the like.

As a spokesman for YouTube notes:

"We take copyright issues very seriously. We prohibit users from uploading infringing material, and we cooperate with all copyright holders to identify and promptly remove infringing content."

YouTube's history of cooperation does not change its "beg for forgiveness" approach—only taking videos off the site when a complaint is filed. That is, the site is not proactive in policing potentially infringing content and has no current means of automatically verifying that an uploaded video is legal. By remaining relatively passive in how it deals with the copyright issue, YouTube is at risk for lawsuits from the holders of those infringed copyrights—especially as the site begins to generate higher revenues and real profits.

Several lawsuits have already been filed. In June 2006, television journalist Robert Tur (also owner of the Los Angeles News Service) sued YouTube for hosting clips from several of his reports, including footage of the beating of trucker Reginald Denny during the 1992 Los Angeles riots. Tur is seeking $150,000 for each of his videos found on the site; the case is still in process.

Even more ominous, in March 2007 Viacom sued YouTube for $1 billion, charging massive copyright infringement from YouTube's posting of more than 100,000 Viacom video clips. Both the lawsuit and the requested financial damages, however, have struck many experts as being on the frivolous side. First, YouTube dutifully complied with Viacom's request to pull its videos from the site, which appears to fulfill YouTube's obligations under the Digital Millennium Copyright Act of 1998. Second, the $1 billion figure is laughably large, especially considering that YouTube itself generated only about $15 million or so in revenues in 2006. Even if Viacom is looking at the $1.65 billion that Google paid for the company and wanting a share of that, there's no way that Viacom's clips accounted for more than half of all YouTube downloads. To me this lawsuit appears to be a negotiating ploy for Viacom in an attempt to get its videos on YouTube and get paid for them—no doubt at a relatively hefty rate. This doesn't mean that it won't ultimately be harmful for YouTube (probably in some sort of pre-trial settlement with Viacom), but it certainly doesn't foretell the end of YouTube as we know it. (YouTube's parent, Google, does have deep pockets, after all.)

Of course, not every media company views YouTube's video file sharing as a threat. Some companies view the proliferation of video clips online as free promotion, which makes them less likely to sue YouTube over illegally uploaded clips. As Sean McManus, president of CBS News and Sports, noted in a July 2006 CBS PublicEye report:

"You've got to find the fine line between the great promotion YouTube gives a network, and protecting our rights. Our inclination now is, the more exposure we get from clips like that, the better it is for CBS News and the CBS television network."

Antipiracy Software

YouTube's liability should decrease as it becomes more proactive in identifying infringing videos—that is, as the site itself identifies illegal videos without waiting for third-party complaints to be filed. This is the direction in which YouTube is moving.

As of October 2006, YouTube is employing antipiracy software that uses audio-signature technology to spot low-quality copies of licensed music videos. This software is used in conjunction with YouTube's agreements with major record labels; when an illegal copy of a music video is found, YouTube is contractually obligated to either remove the copy or replace it with an approved version of the clip.

The problem with this approach, as some see it, is that the antipiracy software is only used when YouTube has a formal licensing agreement with a record label. Thus the site discriminates between those copyright holders with whom it has a formal business agreement and those with whom it doesn't. In other words, YouTube is only protecting selected copyrights, which doesn't sit well with those companies with whom YouTube doesn't yet have a licensing agreement.

As a spokesperson for Viacom noted in a February 2007 Reuters article, YouTube's "proposition that they will only protect copyrighted content when there's a business deal in place is unacceptable." Another industry source likened YouTube's antipiracy policy to a "mafia shakedown." That's probably not the best way to make friends with those in the media industry. (And why YouTube says it will eventually make its antipiracy software available to all content owners.)

Avoiding Copyright Problems

Big-time legal issues aside, how does the copyright issue affect you as a YouTube user?

First, if you're just a viewer, you're in no harm whatsoever. You can't be sued for watching infringing videos, so the only impact is on what videos are available to watch.

Uploaders, however, are affected by this issue. Not only do copyright concerns impact what videos you can upload, it's also possible that you could be held legally liable for uploading illegally copied content. Although that's not a big concern just yet, it's still possible that copyright holders could come after you as well as going after YouTube. It's certainly happened with audio file sharing; the Recording Industry Association of America (RIAA) has been aggressively pursuing legal action against individual file uploaders.

The threat of lawsuits aside, it's more likely that YouTube will take its own action against serial copyright infringers, in the form of terminating your account. That's right; post illegally copied videos to YouTube, and you could be barred from the site.

YouTube's Terms of Use

So what exactly can you upload to YouTube—and what shouldn't you upload?

The first thing any video uploader should do is read YouTube's official terms of use, which you can find at www.youtube.com/t/terms. The relevant parts of this agreement are found in section 5.C., which reads in part:

> *In connection with User Submissions, you further agree that you will not: (i) submit material that is copyrighted, protected by trade secret or otherwise subject to third party proprietary rights, including privacy and publicity rights, unless you are the owner of such rights or have permission from their rightful owner to post the material and to grant YouTube all of the license rights granted herein; (ii) publish falsehoods or misrepresentations that could damage YouTube or any third party; (iii) submit material that is unlawful, obscene, defamatory, libelous, threatening, pornographic, harassing, hateful, racially or ethnically offensive, or encourages conduct that would be considered a criminal offense, give rise to civil liability, violate any law, or is otherwise inappropriate; (iv) post advertisements or solicitations of business: (v) impersonate another person. YouTube does not endorse any User Submission or any opinion, recommendation, or advice expressed therein, and YouTube expressly disclaims any and all liability in connection with User Submissions. YouTube does not permit copyright infringing activities and infringement of intellectual property rights on its Website, and YouTube will remove all Content and User Submissions if properly notified that such Content or User Submission infringes on another's intellectual property rights. YouTube reserves the right to remove Content and User Submissions without prior notice. YouTube will also terminate a User's access to its Website, if they are determined to be a repeat infringer. A repeat infringer is a User who has been notified of*

infringing activity more than twice and/or has had a User Submission removed from the Website more than twice. YouTube also reserves the right to decide whether Content or a User Submission is appropriate and complies with these Terms of Service for violations other than copyright infringement and violations of intellectual property law, such as, but not limited to, pornography, obscene or defamatory material, or excessive length. YouTube may remove such User Submissions and/or terminate a User's access for uploading such material in violation of these Terms of Service at any time, without prior notice and at its sole discretion.

Got all that? In essence, this passage says that you will not knowingly upload videos that contain copyrighted material, and if you do, YouTube will remove that content. YouTube will also terminate your access to the site if you get caught uploading infringing material more than twice. As you might suspect, YouTube reserves the right to decide which content is allowable—and which isn't.

 I am not a lawyer, nor do I play one in a YouTube video. The concepts expressed in this section are for informational purposes only and are not to be considered legal advice. For legal advice, consult a lawyer.

What You Can't Upload

In practical terms, this means that you shouldn't upload any of the following:

- Recordings of television shows (including prime time shows, news broadcasts, sporting events, and the like)
- Clips from commercial DVDs (including movies, music videos, documentaries, and so on)
- Movie trailers
- Music videos
- Recordings of live concerts, including recordings you make yourself with a camcorder

- Home movies or videos that contain commercially available music, even if used as background music
- Home movies or videos that contain other copyrighted videos in the background, or as part of the movie
- Commercials
- Photo montages or slideshows that contain photos taken by someone other than yourself

Sound like a pretty broad list? It is; if held strictly to these guidelines, the vast majority of YouTube videos would be found to be infringing. Which means, of course, that there are a lot of infringing videos online that nobody is getting upset about and that YouTube isn't blocking. Still, you need to be aware that you *could* be infringing if you post videos that meet these criteria, and you could have those videos removed from the YouTube site.

So what videos are completely safe to upload? You should be safe in uploading your own home movies or self-produced videos, as long as no copyrighted material (such as background music) is contained within. You're also safe in uploading recordings and clips that contain copyrighted material as long as you get prior permission to use that material.

Past that, it's always a judgment call.

 It doesn't matter how old or how new a clip is, how long or short it is, or where you obtained it. Even if you copied the clip from another website, if it contains copyrighted material, you still need the copyright holder's permission to upload the clip to YouTube.

Including Music in Your Videos—Legally

Want to include background music in your videos, but don't want to infringe on anyone's copyrights? Then check out YouTube's new AudioSwap feature, currently testing as part of the TestTube incubator. AudioSwap is a collection of music that YouTube has licensed from artists and record labels for use in users' videos. To check it out, go to the AudioSwap page (www.youtube.com/audioswap_main) and click the Try It Out button.

When AudioSwap moves out of the testing phase, the Replace Audio button should be available from the normal Edit My Videos page.

This displays your Edit My Videos page, but with a Replace Audio button added to each video. Click the Replace Audio button, and YouTube displays the AudioSwap page shown in Figure 11.1. Select a Genre, Artist, and Track for your soundtrack, and then listen to the preview of your video with the new soundtrack. If you like what you hear, click the Publish Video button; this republishes your video on the YouTube site, with your original soundtrack replaced by the new soundtrack.

 When you use AudioSwap, your entire original soundtrack is replaced by the selected music. Don't use this feature if you want to keep your original sound—including any dialog!

Figure 11.1
Using YouTube's AudioSwap to add legal music to a video.

Fair Use

There is one major exception to the prohibition against uploading copyrighted material to YouTube. The Fair Use provision of the Federal Copyright Act could exempt you from YouTube's rules and allow certain copyrighted material to be used without the copyright holder's permission. It all depends on how "fair use" is defined.

The principle of fair use goes like this. You are entitled to freely use portions of copyrighted works for purposes of commentary and criticism, without prior approval of the copyright holder. For example, if you want to post a movie review to your blog, you can quote a few lines of dialog from the movie within your review without fearing a lawsuit from the movie studio. You cannot reproduce the entire script, however; that wouldn't be fair use.

The problem with fair use is that there are no hard-and-fast rules as to what constitutes fair use. If the copyright owner disagrees with your interpretation of the concept, you'll end up deciding who's right in a court of law.

How do you determine fair use? According to the Copyright Act, four factors should be considered:

- The purpose and character of the use
- The nature of the copyrighted work
- The amount and substantiality of the portion used
- The effect of the use on the potential market for or value of the copyrighted work

Not very clear, is it? Perhaps the best rule is that if you're in doubt, don't do it. That's the safest course of action.

What to Do If YouTube Pulls One of Your Videos

Okay, so you ignore all the information in this chapter (as most YouTubers do), upload a video to YouTube that contains copyrighted material, and have the bad luck to have the copyright holder notice your video. When the copyright holder files a complaint with YouTube, what happens next?

Let's be honest. YouTube isn't very discerning when it receives this type of complaint. More often than not, YouTube pulls the video without blinking twice—and without investigating the merits of the complaint. This means that it's possible that a perfectly legal video could be removed by YouTube, if a complaint has been mistakenly made.

Info 4U When Viacom demanded that YouTube remove 100,000 or so of the company's videos from its site, several legitimate videos got caught up in the purge. For example, a home video titled "Sunday Night Dinner at Redbones in Somerville, Mass" was mistakenly identified by Viacom as infringing on its copyrights, even though it contained no infringing material. (My guess is that "Somerville Redbones" was too close, semantically, to "Sumner Redstone," the chairman of Viacom.)

When a video of yours receives a copyright infringement complaint, YouTube removes the video from the site and sends you a notice via email. The notice reads something like this:

Dear Member:

This is to notify you that we have removed or disabled access to the following material as a result of a third-party notification by Viacom International Inc. claiming that this material is infringing:

Name of video

Please Note: Repeat incidents of copyright infringement will result in the deletion of your account and all videos uploaded to that account. In order to avoid future strikes against your account, please delete any videos to which you do not own the rights, and refrain from uploading additional videos that infringe on the copyrights of others. For more information about YouTube's copyright policy, please read the Copyright Tips guide.

If you elect to send us a counter notice, to be effective it must be a written communication provided to our designated agent that includes substantially the following (please consult your legal counsel or see 17 U.S.C. Section 512(g)(3) to confirm these requirements):

A physical or electronic signature of the subscriber.

Identification of the material that has been removed or to which access has been disabled and the location at which the material appeared before it was removed or access to it was disabled.

A statement under penalty of perjury that the subscriber has a good faith belief that the material was removed or disabled as a result of mistake or misidentification of the material to be removed or disabled.

The subscriber's name, address, and telephone number, and a statement that the subscriber consents to the jurisdiction of Federal District Court for the judicial district in which the address is located, or if the subscriber's address is outside of the United States, for any judicial district in which the service provider may be found, and that the subscriber will accept service of process from the person who provided notification under subsection (c)(1)(C) or an agent of such person.

Such written notice should be sent to our designated agent as follows:

DMCA Complaints
YouTube, Inc.
1000 Cherry Ave.
Second Floor
San Bruno, CA 94066
Email: copyright@youtube.com

Please note that under Section 512(f) of the Copyright Act, any person who knowingly materially misrepresents that material or activity was removed or disabled by mistake or misidentification may be subject to liability.

Sincerely,
YouTube, Inc.

What can you do if you receive such a notice that your video has been removed from YouTube? As the message states, your recourse is to respond to YouTube's DMCA Complaints department, either via email or snail mail. You'll need to provide proof of why your video isn't infringing and be prepared for some drawn-out back and for-thing with YouTube over the video in question. And there's no guarantee that YouTube will buy your argument and repost the video; as I said earlier, YouTube is very cooperative with the big copyright holders, and not so much with individual users.

DMCA stands for the Digital Millennium Copyright Act, a 1998 bill that updates previous United States copyright law for the electronic age. Learn more about DMCA and copyright issues at the U.S. Copyright Office website (www.copyright.gov/legislation/dmca.pdf), the Electronic Frontier Foundation (www.eff.org/IP/DMCA/), and the Anti-DMCA Website (www.anti-dmca.org).

What's Yours Is Theirs: Controlling Use of Your Own Videos

Problems can also arise when you upload your own private videos to YouTube and other people appropriate them for their own use. These are copyright problems of another sort, especially if you don't want other users copying or otherwise using your videos without your consent. Unfortunately, as soon as you upload a video to YouTube, you lose most control over what happens with that video.

Who Owns Your Videos?

Let's be clear. You retain the copyright for any video you create, even if you upload to YouTube or another file sharing site. Just because a video is posted publicly does not mean that is in the public domain; as YouTube states in section 5.B. of its Terms of Use:

For clarity, you retain all of your ownership rights in your User Submissions.

That does not mean, however, that you can control how your video is used, especially on the YouTube site. In fact, YouTube's Terms of Use goes on to say, in the very next sentence:

However, by submitting the User Submissions to YouTube, you hereby grant YouTube a worldwide, non-exclusive, royalty-free, sublicenseable and transferable license to use, reproduce, distribute, prepare derivative works of, display, and perform the User Submissions in connection with the YouTube Website and YouTube's (and its successor's) business, including without limitation for promoting and redistributing part or all of the YouTube Website (and derivative works thereof) in any media formats and through any media channels. You also hereby grant each user of the YouTube Website a non-exclusive license to access your User Submissions through the Website, and to use, reproduce, distribute, prepare derivative works of, display and perform such User Submissions as permitted through the functionality of the Website and under these Terms of Service.

In other words, any video you upload to YouTube can be used by YouTube in any way it sees fit, no approval required on your part. In addition, any other user of YouTube can also use your video in any way desired, again with no approval necessary. You may own the rights, but YouTube and its millions of users can access, use, reproduce, or distribute your video, no questions asked.

What does this mean? It means that if YouTube wanted to create a DVD of your videos, it could. If YouTube wanted to base a television show on your videos, it could. If YouTube wanted to publish a book containing screenshots from your videos, it could. As could any of YouTube's users. And they wouldn't have to pay you a penny to do any of these things.

That's right, when you upload a video to YouTube, you grant YouTube and its users a license to use your material, free of charge. It's still your material, but they can use it as they wish—and have no obligation to compensate you for its use.

There's nothing you can do about this, however, save for not uploading your videos to YouTube in the first place. But it's something you need to know.

 The nonexclusive license you grant to YouTube and its users exists only as long as your video resides on the YouTube site. If you remove your video from YouTube, the license terminates, and all rights revert back to you, the copyright holder.

Reporting Copyright Violations

Then there's the issue of someone literally stealing your video—uploading a video to which you own the copyright, without your permission.

As noted previously in this chapter, YouTube is sympathetic to copyright violation complaints. All you have to do is file a complaint with YouTube, and chances are the offending video will be removed.

How do you file a copyright violation complaint? You need to send a formal notification to YouTube's DMCA Complaints department, either via email or postal mail, at the following address:

DMCA Complaints
YouTube, Inc.
1000 Cherry Ave.
Second Floor
San Bruno, CA 94066
Fax: 650.872.8513
Email: copyright@youtube.com

Your complaint should contain the following:

- A physical or electronic signature of a person authorized to act on behalf of the copyright owner (that's either you or your lawyer)

- Identification of the copyrighted work(s) that you think have been infringed

- Identification of the material that you claim is infringing on your copyrighted material, ideally in the form of URLs for the offending videos

- Your name, address, telephone number, and email address (or the same information for your lawyer)

- A statement that you have a good faith belief that use of the material on YouTube is not authorized by you, your agents, or the law

- A statement that the information in the notification is accurate and, under penalty of perjury, that you or your lawyer is authorized to act on behalf of the owner of an exclusive right that is allegedly infringed

The best way to proceed is to email all this information to YouTube, making sure to include the offending videos' URLs in the body of your email message. This way YouTube can quickly act to remove the identified videos, without waiting for the postal service to do its thing.

YouTube 4 Advanced Users

Joining the YouTube Community—And Creating Your Own Channel

YouTube is a video sharing community. The community aspects of the site let you share your videos with others, identify others who share your particular interests, and even communicate with other users. When you join the YouTube community, you'll get a lot more out of the site—and find more fun videos to watch!

Working with Channels

The most common way to participate in the YouTube community is by utilizing YouTube's *channels*. On YouTube, a channel is just a fancy name for a user's profile. Other users can access your channel/profile to find out what videos you've uploaded and which videos are your favorites; you can also subscribe to a user's profile to be notified when that user uploads new videos to the YouTube site.

Viewing a Channel Profile

You access a user's channel by clicking on that user's name wherever it appears on the YouTube site. This takes you to the user's channel/profile page, like the one shown in Figure 12.1. Although each profile page is unique, all pages contain the same major elements:

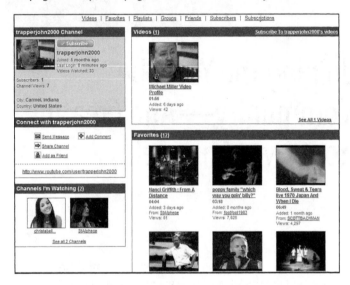

Figure 12.1
A typical YouTube channel profile page.

- Links to the user's favorite videos, playlists, groups, friends, and the like
- Information about the user, including a link to subscribe to this channel
- Videos uploaded by this user
- Links to connect to the user, via email, comments, and so on
- The user's favorite videos
- Channels the user is watching
- Subscribers to the user's channel
- Comments on this user's channel

In other words, you access a user's channel page to learn more about that user—and to connect with that person.

Subscribing to a Channel

If you like what you see on a user's channel/profile page, you can *subscribe* to that person's channel. When you subscribe to a channel, you are automatically notified (via email) when the user uploads new videos.

To subscribe to a user's channel, go that person's channel/profile page and click the Subscribe button. To unsubscribe to a channel, return to that user's channel/profile page and click the Un-Subscribe button. To view videos from your currently subscribed-to channels, go to YouTube's home page and click the Subscriptions link in the My box.

 YouTube thrives on social networking—and your channel and videos will get more viewers if you fully participate in the YouTube community. That means subscribing to a lot of channels and leaving comments with those videos and users you identify with. What goes around comes around; the more comments you leave, the more people will see your name and channel, and the more views your videos will receive.

Personalizing Your YouTube Channel

Because a YouTube channel page is really a user profile page, you'll want to create your own channel page and customize it to reflect your personality. It's easy to do.

As to creating your channel page, there's nothing to do; YouTube creates a profile page for you when you subscribe to the site. The default channel page is a little bland, however—which is why you want to customize it.

You personalize your channel page from your My Account page. Just click the My Account link at the top of any YouTube page, and when the My Account page appears, scroll to the Channel Settings section, shown in Figure 12.2.

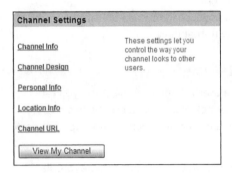

Figure 12.2
Getting ready to personalize your channel profile page.

From here you can edit the following channel elements:

- **Channel Info**—As shown in Figure 12.3, you can enter a new title and description for your channel page. You can also opt to select a new video to use for your profile picture (by default, your last-uploaded video serves this function), as well as configure other channel display options.

- **Channel Design**—As shown in Figure 12.4, this is where you change the overall look and feel of your channel page. You can select a new color scheme for your page; opt to show or hide various page elements; and choose custom colors for selected page elements, as well as a background image for your page.

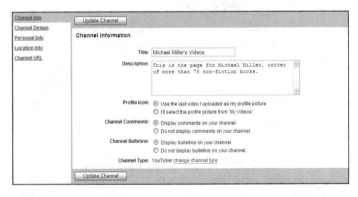

Figure 12.3
Personalizing your channel info.

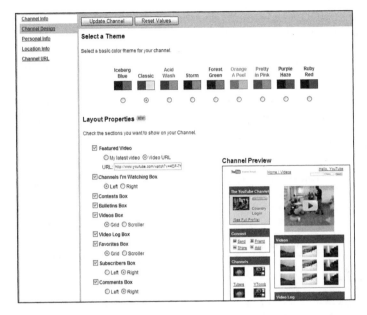

Figure 12.4
Personalizing the design of your channel page.

- **Personal Info**—As shown in Figure 12.5, this page lets you enter personal information to be displayed on your channel page, such as your name, gender, description of yourself, link to an outside website, occupation, interests, and so on.
- **Location Info**—As shown in Figure 12.6, this is where you enter your hometown, current city, Zip code, and country.
- **Channel URL**—As shown in Figure 12.7, this page displays the URL for your channel page.

As you make changes to any page element, make sure you click the Update Channel button—or you'll lose the changes you made.

 To hide your age on your channel/profile page, go to your My Account page, scroll to the Channel Settings section, click the Personal Info link, and then select the Do Not Display Your Age on Your Public Profile option. Click the Update Channel button when finished.

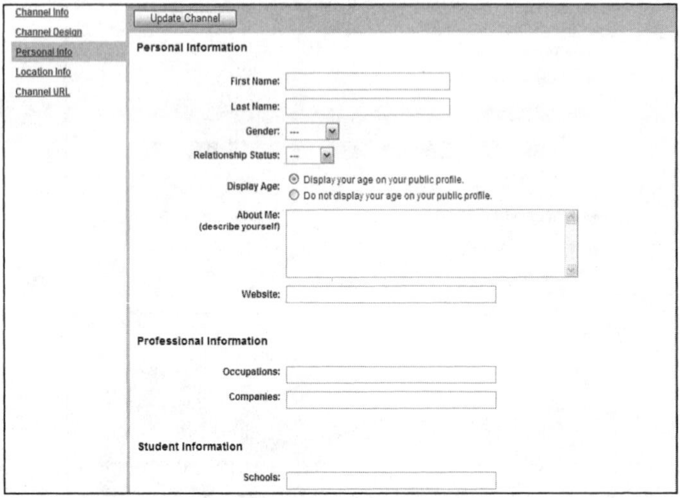

Figure 12.5
Adding personal info to your channel page.

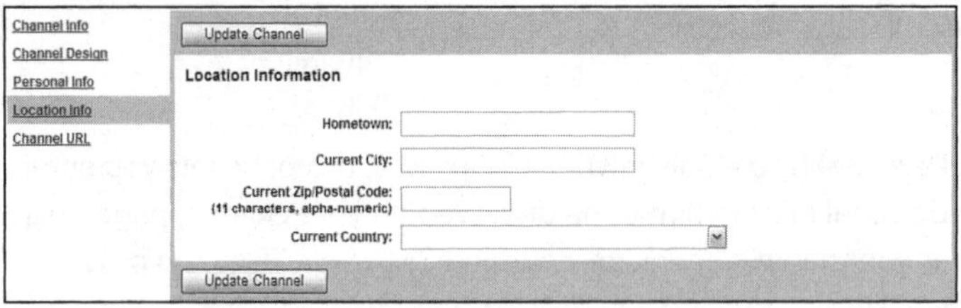

Figure 12.6
Adding your location to your channel page.

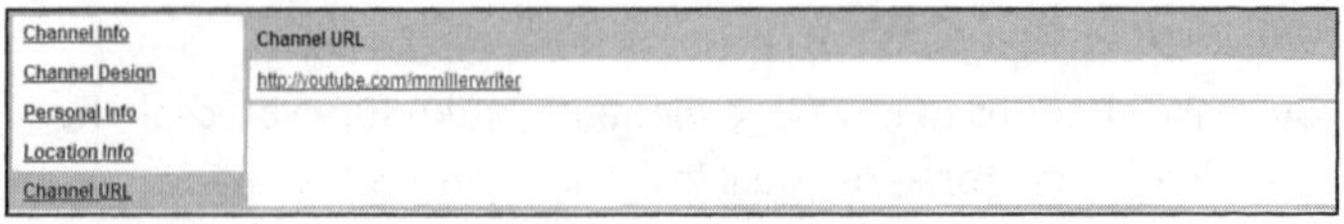

Figure 12.7
Viewing your channel URL.

Managing Your Channel's Video Blog

One cool feature that you can add to your channel page is a video blog, or *Vlog*. A Vlog is an easy way for you to create a personal video journal accessible to anyone visiting your channel.

To create a Vlog, go to the YouTube home page and click the Playlists link in the My box. When the Playlists page appears, you can choose to select an existing playlist as your Vlog, or create a new playlist to hold new Vlog entries. To use an existing playlist, select the playlist and then click the Set as Vlog button. To create a new Vlog playlist, click the Create Playlist button to create the new playlist, and make sure you check the Use This Playlist as Video Log in My Channel option.

Your Vlog now appears on your channel profile page. The individual videos in the Vlog playlist are stacked on top of each other; visitors can click a video to view it.

Working with Groups

Another form of community on YouTube is the YouTube groups feature. A group is a social forum where users interested in a given topic can share videos and conduct online discussions.

Joining an Existing Group

To find YouTube groups, click the Community tab and then click the Groups link on the left side of the page. You can now browse groups by type (Featured, Recently Added, Most Members, Most Videos, Most Discussions, or Colleges) or by Categories.

When you access a group page, like the one shown in Figure 12.8, you see links to group videos, members, and discussions. Recent videos are displayed, as are the most recent group discussions.

To join a group, simply click the Join This Group link. After you've joined a group, you can participate in group discussions, add videos to the group, and so forth.

Joining a group discussion is as easy as clicking the discussion link; this displays the discussion page, such as the one shown in Figure 12.9. You can then read comments within that discussion, or add your own comment from the Add New Comment section at the bottom of the page.

Figure 12.8
A YouTube group page.

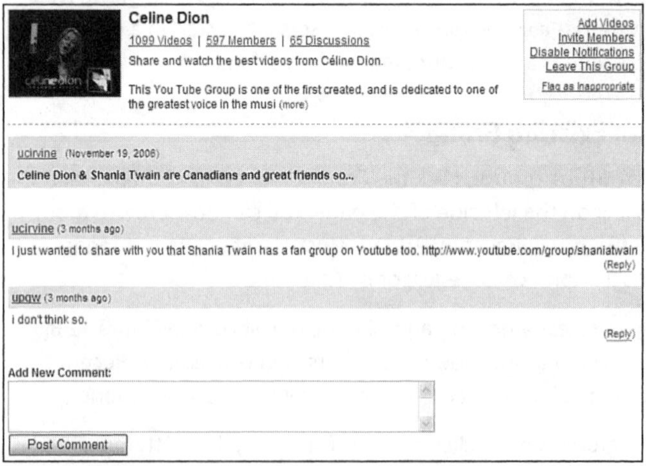

Figure 12.9
Joining in a group discussion.

Joining a College Group

YouTube also has special groups for selected colleges. Click the Colleges link on the Community page to display the Colleges page, shown in Figure 12.10. From here you can select your college from the Join Your College list; then click the Join Now button. (You'll need to enter your college email address to join your college group; this keeps nonstudents from participating.)

Figure 12.10
Joining a college group.

Creating a New Group

You can also create your own personal YouTube group about any topic you want. Just click the Groups link on the Community page; then click the Create a Group button. When the Create a Group page appears, as shown in Figure 12.11, enter a name and description for the group, along with identifying tags, a custom URL for the group, a category, the type of group (public or private), and how you want to handle video uploads, forum postings, and the group icon. Click the Create Group button when finished, and your group is launched into the YouTube community.

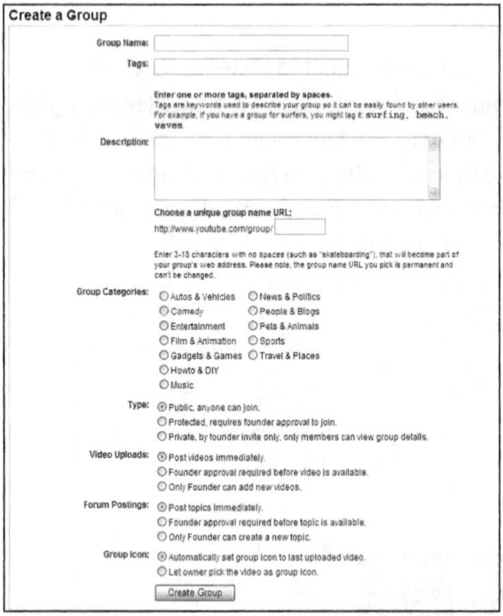

Figure 12.11
Creating a new YouTube Group.

To invite others to join your group, click the Invite Members link at the top right of the group page. This displays the page shown in Figure 12.12; you can invite members of your Friends list, or invite other members by entering their member names in the New Friends list. Click the Send button to send your invitations.

To add videos to your group, click the Add Videos link at the top right of the group page. This displays a page with links to your current favorite videos and playlists, as shown in Figure 12.13. Check any video you want to add; then click the Add to Group button. Alternatively, you can click the Upload a Video button to upload a new video and add it to your group.

Figure 12.12
Inviting other YouTubers to join your group.

Figure 12.13
Adding videos to your new group.

Working with Friends and Contacts

You don't have to create a group to mingle with people on YouTube. That's because YouTube lets you create lists of users with whom you can share your videos. These Friends and Family lists are kind of like the Buddy lists in AOL Instant Messenger; one click on a YouTube list lets you share your videos.

Adding a Friend to Your List

Adding an existing YouTube member to your friends list is relatively easy. Just go to that member's channel/profile page, scroll to the Connect With box, shown in Figure 12.14, and click the Add as Friend link. You'll now see the Friend Invitation page, shown in Figure 12.15; select whether to add this person as Friends or Family; then click the Send Invite button. The person will receive an email invitation to be your friend; if he accepts, he's added to your friends list.

Figure 12.14
Adding an existing YouTube member to your friends list.

Figure 12.15
Sending the friend's invitation.

You can also add friends who aren't yet YouTube members. Just click the My Account link at the top of any YouTube page to display the My Account page; then scroll down to the Friends & Contacts section, shown in Figure 12.16, and click the Invite More Friends button. When the Invite Your Friends page appears, as shown in Figure 12.17, enter your name, the email addresses of those folks you want to invite (separate each address with a comma), and a personal invitation message. Click the Send Invite button, and your friends will receive an official email invitation. They can click the link in the email message to join YouTube and be added to your friends list.

Figure 12.16
Managing friends and contacts from your My Account page.

Figure 12.17
Inviting a non-YouTuber to join your friends list.

You're not limited to just two contact lists (Friends and Family). To create new lists, go to your All Contacts page, click the Create New List button, and then enter a name for the list. You can then move existing contacts to the new list by checking a contact name and selecting the new list from the Copy Contacts To list.

Sending Messages to Your Friends

When you want to send a message to someone in your friends list, go to your My Account page, scroll down to the Friends & Contacts section, and click the All Contacts link. As you can see in Figure 12.18, this lists all your contacts, no matter which list you've put them in. Click the Send Message link next to a friend's name; this displays the Compose Message page shown in Figure 12.19. Enter a subject for your message and the text of the message itself. If you want to attach a YouTube video to this message, pull down the Attach a Video list and choose a video from your favorites. Click the Send Message button to send the message on its way.

 You're not limited to sending messages only to existing friends and contacts. To send a message to any YouTube user, go to your inbox and click the Compose New Message button; from here you can enter any member's username for the message you compose.

Figure 12.18
Viewing all your YouTube contacts.

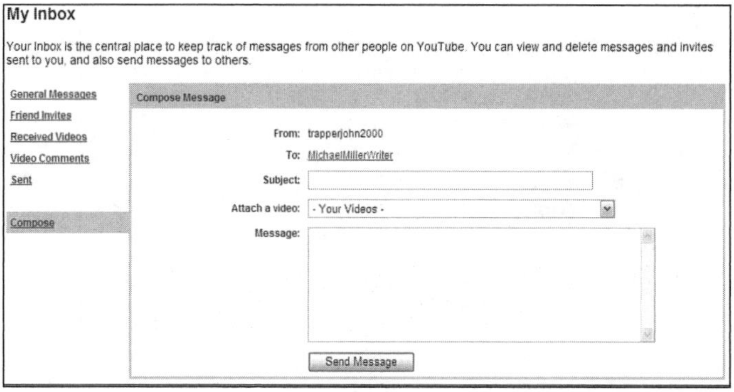

Figure 12.19
Sending a message to a friend.

Reading Messages from Other Users

Messages sent to you from other users end up in your YouTube inbox. You access the inbox from YouTube's home page; just click the Inbox link in the My box. As you can see in Figure 12.20, your inbox lists all email messages you've received, under the General Messages link. (You can view other types of messages by clicking the Friend Invites, Received Videos, Video Comments, Video Responses, or Sent links.)

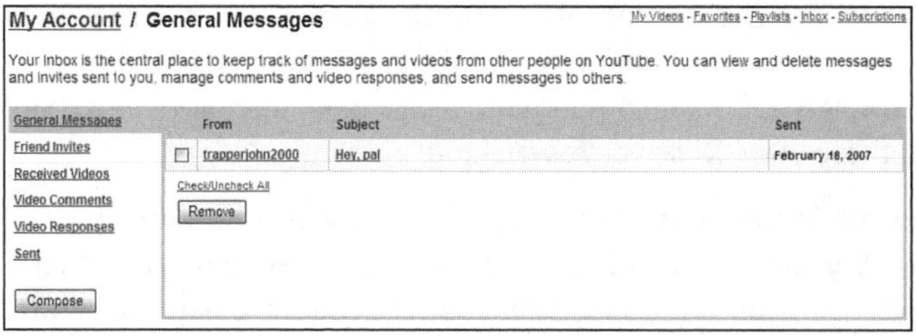

Figure 12.20
Waiting messages in your YouTube inbox.

To read a message, just click it in your inbox. The message is now displayed onscreen, as shown in Figure 12.21. You can delete the message, mark it as spam, or send a reply to the message by using the Your Reply box and the Send Message button.

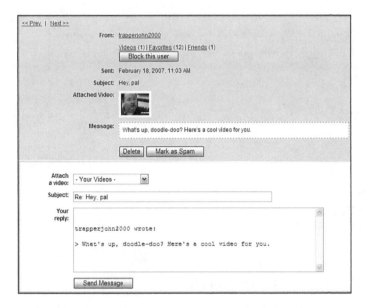

Figure 12.21
Reading a message from another user.

Chatting with Other Users Via Streams

Another way to participate in the YouTube community is to chat with other viewers in real-time, using YouTube's new Streams feature. Streams lets you watch a video with a group of other users, and chat with those users while you're watching.

The main Streams page, shown in Figure 12.22, lists the currently active Streams. To join a Stream, simply click the Stream name. Alternatively, you can start a new Stream by clicking the Create Your Own Stream link.

When you join a Stream, you see a page like the one shown in Figure 12.23. The currently playing video is shown in the main video player window; the other users in the Stream are listed to the right of the video; chat comments are listed even farther right; and the playlist of videos in the Stream is displayed above all. Enter your chat messages in the message box on the bottom right; press the Enter button to post your message. It's a fun way to watch videos as a group!

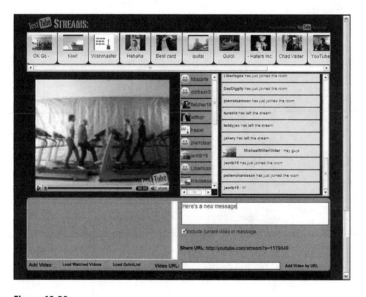

Figure 12.22
Viewing YouTube Streams.

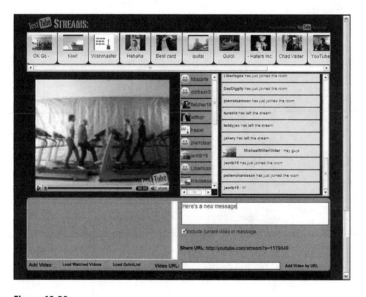

Figure 12.23
Chatting about videos in a YouTube Stream.

 As of spring 2007, Streams is currently in the public testing phase as part of YouTube's TestTube program. To check it out, go to www.youtube.com/streams_main.

Keeping in Touch Via the YouTube Blog and Forum

Want to keep up with what's going on behind the scenes at YouTube? Want to get to know some of the people who make the site work? Then check out the YouTube blog, shown in Figure 12.24. The YouTube Blog is a collection of text and video posts by members of the YouTube team. It's a great way to put faces to the services offered by the YouTube site.

Figure 12.24
YouTube's internal community—the YouTube Blog.

You access the YouTube Blog at www.youtube.com/blog, or by clicking the Blog link at the bottom of any YouTube page.

Also interesting are the Unofficial YouTube Forums (www.youtubeforums.com), shown in Figure 12.25. At the name implies, this is an unofficial site where people gather to discuss all things YouTube. It's a great place to hang out with fellow YouTubers, ask questions of more experienced users, share links to cool videos you've seen, promote your own videos, and just generally chat about what you do or don't like about YouTube.

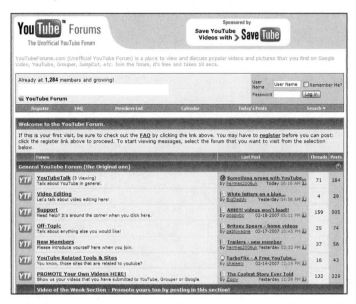

Figure 12.25
Chat with fellow YouTubers at the Unofficial YouTube Forums.

Adding YouTube Videos to Your Own Site or Blog

One of the great things about YouTube is how easy it is to share YouTube videos. You've already learned how to share videos via email links; now it's time to learn how to share videos via your own web page or blog.

Adding YouTube Video Links to a Web Page

The easiest way to reference a YouTube video is via a link to that video page on the YouTube site. Every YouTube video has its own unique URL; you can copy and paste this URL into email messages, newsgroup postings, or your own web page.

Linking to an Individual Video

You can find a video's link URL in the information box at the top right of the video page, as shown in Figure 13.1. It's the bit in the URL box, just below the video's tags.

 To insert a YouTube video link into an email message, simply copy the URL from the video page and paste it into the body of your email message.

Figure 13.1
The URL and embed links for a typical YouTube video.

To insert the link into a web page, copy it from the video page and insert it into your page's underlying HTML code, surrounding by the appropriate link tag. The resulting code should look something like this:

```
Click <a href="http//:www.youtube.com/watch?v=12345">
here</a> to view my YouTube video.
```

Naturally, replace the href link with the URL from the video you're linking to. The resulting text and link should look like that shown in Figure 13.2. When visitors click the link in the text, they're taken to that video's YouTube page.

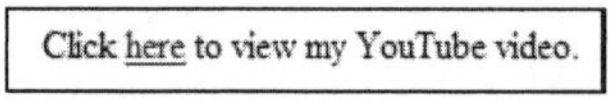

Figure 13.2
A link to a YouTube video inserted into a typical web page.

Linking to Your Profile Page—Or List of Videos

YouTube also lets you link to your YouTube profile page. Just use this URL within your link code:

```
http://www.youtube.com/user/username
```

Alternatively, you can link to a list of your uploaded videos, using this URL:

```
http://www.youtube.com/videos/username
```

In both instances, replace *username* with your YouTube username.

You can also link to any playlist you've created. Just go to your My Playlists page, select the playlist, and copy the URL in the URL box. (To embed all the videos in a playlist, copy the Embed link instead.)

Embedding YouTube Videos in a Web Page

Linking to YouTube videos from your web page is one thing; embedding an actual video into your web page is quite another. That's right, YouTube lets you insert any of its public videos into your own web page, complete with video player window. And it's easy to do.

That's because YouTube automatically creates the embed code for every public video on its site (as well as your own private videos), and lists this code on the video page itself. The code is in the information box at the top right of the video page, just below the URL code. You'll need to copy this entire code (it's longer than the Embed box itself) and then paste it into the HTML code on your website.

The embed code, when properly formatted, looks something like this:

```
<object width="425" height="350">
    <param name="movie" value="http://www.youtube.com/
    v/12345"></param>
    <param name="wmode" value="transparent"></param>
    <embed src="http://www.youtube.com/v/12345"
    type="application/x-shockwave-flash"
    wmode="transparent" width="425" height="350">
    </embed>
</object>
```

 Don't copy *this* code to your web page—it's just an example!

Insert this code into your web page's HTML, where you want the video player window to display. What you get is a special click-to-play YouTube video player window, like the one shown in Figure 13.3, in line on your web page. The video itself remains stored on and served from YouTube's servers; only the code resides on your website. When a site visitor clicks the video, it's served from YouTube's servers to your viewer's web browser, just as if it were served from your own server. (This means you don't waste any of your own storage space or bandwidth on the video.)

 To turn a click-to-play video into an autoplay video, insert the following code directly after both instances of the video's URL (no space between and before the end quotation mark): **&autoplay=1**.

Figure 13.3
A click-to-play YouTube video window on your website.

Embedding a Video List in Your Web Page

YouTube also lets you embed a scrolling list of your YouTube videos on your web page, like the one shown in Figure 13.4. Visitors can click on any video in the list to view the video on YouTube.

To create this type of scrolling list, simply insert the following code into your web page HTML:

```
<iframe id="videos_list" name="videos_list"
src="http://www.youtube.com/videos_list?user=username"
scrolling="auto" width="265" height="300" frameborder="0"
marginheight="0" marginwidth="0">
</iframe>
```

Make sure you replace *username* with your own YouTube username.

Figure 13.4
A scrolling list of your YouTube videos for your web page.

Embedding YouTube Videos in Your MySpace Profile

Many MySpace users like to add YouTube videos to their profile pages. Fortunately, MySpace lets you edit the underlying HTML code for this profile page, which is how you embed YouTube videos.

Embedding an Individual Video

There are a few different ways to embed YouTube videos in your MySpace profile page. Perhaps the most common method is to embed a single video on your page. Unfortunately, you can't use YouTube's standard embed code because MySpace doesn't support the `<object>` tag—so you'll need to remove this tag from the regular embed code.

Here's what you do. Start by copying the embed code from the YouTube video page. Next, paste this code into your MySpace profile page HTML. Then delete the starting and ending `<object>` and `</object>` codes, so that the resulting code looks like this:

```
<param name="movie" value="http://www.youtube.com/
v/12345"></param>
<param name="wmode" value="transparent"></param>
<embed src="http://www.youtube.com/v/12345"
type="application/x-shockwave-flash" wmode="transparent"
width="425"
height="350">
</embed>
```

Your YouTube video should now appear on your profile page.

Embedding a List of Your Videos

Alternatively, you can embed a list of your YouTube videos in your MySpace profile page. To do this, add the following code to your profile page HTML:

```
<embed src="http://www.youtube.com/swf_show/username"
quality="high" width="425" height="350" name="myclips"
align="middle" allowScriptAccess="sameDomain"
type="application/x-shockwave-flash"
pluginspage="http://www.macromedia.com/go/getflashplayer" />
```

Replace *username* with your YouTube username, and you'll create the type of scrolling video list shown back in Figure 13.4, but in your MySpace profile page.

Adding YouTube Videos to Your Blog

If you have your own personal blog, YouTube makes it easy to send any public YouTube video to your blog as a blog posting. First, however, you have to tell YouTube about your blog, so it knows where to send the post.

Configuring YouTube for Your Blog

Start by clicking the My Account link at the top of any YouTube page; when the My Account page appears, scroll down to the Account Settings section and click the Video Posting Settings link. This displays the page shown in Figure 13.5; click the Add a Blog/Site button.

 YouTube supports automatic posting to the following blog hosts: Blogger, Friendster, LiveJournal, WordPress.com, and WordPress self-hosted blogs.

Figure 13.5
Getting ready to configure YouTube for your own personal blog.

YouTube now displays the Add a Blog/Site page shown in Figure 13.6. Pull down the Blog Service list and select your blog host; then enter your blog username and password. Click the Add Blog button, and you're finished with this preliminary setup.

Figure 13.6
Adding a blog to your YouTube configuration.

 If you have multiple blogs, you can configure YouTube accordingly. Just repeat this setup procedure for each of the blogs you post to.

Posting a Video to Your Blog

Once configured, it's a snap to send any public YouTube video to your blog. Just open the video page and scroll to the options box below the video player window, shown in Figure 13.7. Click the Post Video link and YouTube displays the Post Video pane shown in Figure 13.8. Choose a blog from the list, enter a title for this post, and then enter any text you want to accompany the video. Click the Post to Blog button, and YouTube posts the video (and accompanying text) to your blog as a new post, like the one shown in Figure 13.9.

 If you have a WordPress blog, you can also embed a YouTube video into your blog using the following code: [youtube=*url*]. Replace *url* with the video's URL, as copied from the video page, and the click-to-play video will be embedded.

Figure 13.7
Click the Post Video link to post this video to your blog.

Figure 13.8
Posting a video to your personal blog.

Figure 13.9
A YouTube video appearing as a Blogger blog post.

 If you're a website developer, YouTube offers a set of tools, called the YouTube Application Programming Interface (API), that lets you develop web-based applications using YouTube videos. Learn more—and access the YouTube API Developer Forum—at www.youtube.com/dev.

Profiting from Your YouTube Videos

If you upload a lot of videos to YouTube, especially videos you produce yourself, you may be wondering whether there's any way to make money from all this activity. The answer is yes—sort of.

Let YouTube Pay You

Here's the reality. At present, YouTube is a true video sharing community—with the emphasis on the word "sharing." And when you share, you give of yourself (and your videos) freely, with no anticipation of profit.

In other words, YouTube doesn't have any means for you to generate revenues from the videos you upload.

Yet.

This situation is due to change, if we're to believe YouTube co-founder Chad Hurley. In January 2007, Hurley announced at the World Economic Forum that YouTube was working on a plan that would let the site share its revenues with its users.

YouTube generates revenues by selling advertising on its pages. Theoretically, any revenue sharing plan would send some portion of these revenues to users who upload videos to the site, when those videos are viewed by other users.

At this point in time it's unknown how a YouTube revenue sharing plan would work. That said, the yet-to-be-finalized plan is expected to employ different types of advertisements, including short clips shown ahead of the actual videos. Obviously, this plan will be available only to users who own full copyright to the videos they upload.

 Look for new news about YouTube's upcoming profit-sharing plan at YouTube's Press Room page (www.youtube.com/press_room).

Use Your YouTube Videos to Promote Other Products and Services

Until YouTube rolls out its revenue sharing plan, you have to be a bit more creative if you want to profit from your YouTube videos.

One way to make money from YouTube videos to use the videos you upload to promote other products or services that you sell. That is, you upload videos that function either as blatant advertisements or infomercials, or as "teasers" for additional services.

Let's say that you offer gift baskets for sale. You create a short video for YouTube about how to make gift baskets and prominently display your web page address or phone number in the video. Because the video has some informational content (the how-to information), it attracts viewers, of which a certain percentage of them will follow through to purchase the gift baskets you have for sale.

 If you have products or services to sell, make sure you put your web page URL in the video's text description—so viewers don't have to rewatch the video to find the ordering info. And make sure you include contact information about your products and services in your YouTube channel profile, as well.

Or maybe you're a business consultant and you want to promote your consulting services. To demonstrate what you have to offer potential clients, you create and upload some sort of short video—a motivational lecture, perhaps, or a slideshow about specific business practices, or something similar. You use the video to establish your expert status and then display your email address or web page URL to solicit business for your consulting services. (Figure 14.1 shows one such video, offering aviation consulting services.)

Figure 14.1
Using a YouTube video to sell consulting services.

Or maybe you have a full-length DVD video for sale. You excerpt a portion of that video and upload it to YouTube, with graphics before and after (and maybe even during) the video detailing how the full-length DVD can be ordered.

Likewise if you're a musician with CDs to sell, an author with books to sell, an artist with paintings or other artwork to sell, or a craftsmaker with various crafts and such to sell. The musician might create a music video to promote his CDs; the author might read an excerpt from her book; the artist might produce a photo slideshow of his work; and the craftsmaker might upload a short video walk-through of pieces she has for sale. Make sure you include details for how the additional product can be ordered, and let your placement on YouTube do the promotion for you.

As an example, Charles Smith Pottery offers a series of instructional videos on YouTube, such as the one shown in Figure 14.2, that demonstrate how to use a pottery wheel. Interested viewers can then access the accompanying website (detailed both in the video and in the video's description) to learn more and to see what products the company has for sale.

Figure 14.2
Using a YouTube video to sell pottery.

Sell Product Placement in Your Videos

Okay, this next idea is a bit of a stretch, but you never know. Just as movie studios and television networks sell product placement in their movies and TV shows, you can sell product placement in your YouTube videos—especially if you have a track record of high viewership.

Although you probably don't have the resources or contacts to sell product placement on your own, you can use the services of Entertainment Media Works (EMW; www.entmediaworks.com), a company that specializes in just such product placement. EMW plans to roll out services based on what it calls *plinking*, or product linking, in consumer-generated media. Plinking is the process of adding a link to a product or service to an object or image in a video; viewers click on the link to learn more about and hopefully place an order for the linked-to product or service.

For example, you might have a video where you're wearing a certain type of jacket. EMW would add a "plink" to the jacket image in certain frames of the video; a viewer would pause the video, click on the jacket, and be taken to the jacket manufacturer's website. If the viewer purchases a jacket, the manufacturer would pay some sort of commission to the video's producer.

Or so it goes in theory. Plinking is still in the concept stage, and other firms haven't yet recognized the potential of product placement in YouTube videos. But expect this to catch on, in various shapes and forms.

Sell Advertising Around Embedded YouTube Videos on Your Own Website

Whereas plinking might be a source of revenues in the future, there is another way to make money from YouTube videos today. All you need is a YouTube video or two, your own website, and a subscription to Google AdSense.

The key to this approach is to generate revenues from your own website, from traffic driven by embedded YouTube videos. The more interesting the videos, the more traffic you'll attract; the more traffic you attract, the more click-throughs you'll get on the ads you place on your site.

Of course, this approach involves signing up for some sort of ad revenue sharing service. The most popular of such services is Google AdSense.

Google's AdSense program places content-targeted ads on your site, sells those ads to appropriate advertisers, monitors visitor click-throughs, tracks how much money is owed you, and then pays you what you've earned. All you have to do is sign up for the program, insert a few lines of code into your web page's underlying HTML code, and then sit back and let Google do the rest of the work.

Because AdSense ads are context-sensitive, the ads served should relate to the content of your videos. For example, if you embed a music video from your favorite band, AdSense might serve up an ad for that band's latest CD. Or if you embed a how-to video that shows how to connect a computer printer, AdSense might serve up an ad for printers or ink cartridges.

Signing up for the Google AdSense program is easy enough to do, and completely free. You start at the main AdSense page (www.google.com/adsense/), shown in Figure 14.3, and then click the Click Here to Apply button. The next page is an application form; fill this in and then let Google review your application. The review period typically runs two to three days, and then Google will notify you of your acceptance and you'll be ready to log in to your AdSense account and get started with the rest of the process.

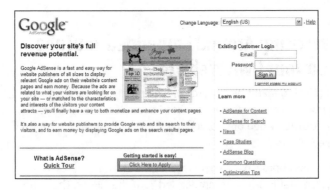

Figure 14.3
Use Google AdSense to generate revenues from YouTube videos embedded in your website.

After your account is approved, you need to add ads to your website. To do this, go to the AdSense home page, click the AdSense for Content link, and then select what type of ad (size and format) you want to insert. Google displays the HTML code for this ad; copy and paste this code into the HTML code for your web page. Your page now displays the ad block, like the one shown in Figure 14.4, with ad content relevant to the YouTube video you've also embedded on the page.

Figure 14.4
A typical block of AdSense ads.

You make money any time someone clicks on the links in the ad. AdSense keeps track of all clicks and issues checks (or deposits to your bank account) on a monthly basis.

Clickers don't have to purchase anything for you to generate revenues from your ads. AdSense operates on a pay-
per-click basis.

Ditch YouTube for a For-Profit Video Sharing Site

Given that YouTube doesn't (yet) pay you for the videos you post on
its site, you might want to turn to a site that does. That's right, several
video sharing sites on the web are also revenue sharing sites; when
visitors view your videos, these sites pay you money.

Making Money with Revver

One such site is Revver (www.revver.com), shown in Figure 14.5.
Revver inserts advertisements onto user-submitted videos, and then
pays users a share of the profits from those ads. The more viewers a
video has, the more money you'll make.

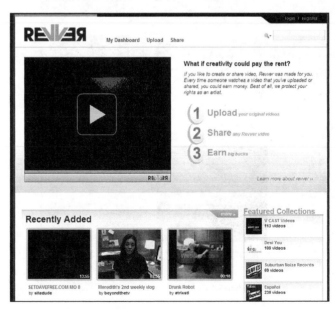

Figure 14.5
Revver, a video and revenue sharing site.

Revver splits ad revenues 50/50. So, for example, if a given ad attached to a video generates $100 in click-through revenues, you'll get $50. You can even make money by embedding Revver videos on your website; when you share videos in this way, you earn 20% of ad revenue generated.

 Revver isn't just a web-only service. It recently signed a deal with Verizon to deliver video clips to that company's cell phone subscribers.

Making Money with Flixya

Flixya (www.flixya.com), shown in Figure 14.6, is a similar video/revenue sharing community. Like Revver, Flixya shares ad revenues on a 50/50 basis. Unlike Revver, Flixya uses Google AdSense to serve ads on its video pages; it also offers a way to send your proceeds to the charity of your choice.

Figure 14.6
Another video/revenue sharing site: Flixya.

Making Money with Metacafe

Another website that offers video sharing is Metacafe (www.
metacafe.com), shown in Figure 14.7. Metacafe's Producer Rewards
program is relatively simple; you earn $5 for every 1,000 views of your
video—although payment doesn't start until you've reached 20,000
views ($100).

Figure 14.7
Earn $5 per 1,000 views on Metacafe.

Making Money with Break.com

The Break.com website (www.break.com) offers a slightly different
way to make money from your uploaded videos. This site, shown in
Figure 14.8, doesn't share revenues, but does pay for its most popular
original videos. In particular, Break.com will pay you $25 if your video
is featured in a gallery, and from $400 to $2,000 if your video is featured on the site's home page.

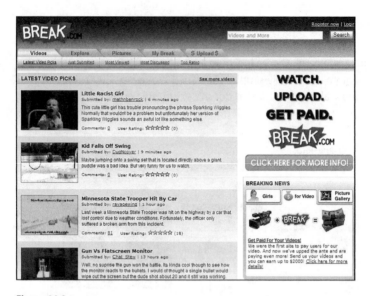

Figure 14.8
Break.com pays for the best original videos featured on its site.

How to Increase Your YouTube Ratings— And Your Potential Profits

If and when YouTube ever starts sharing revenues with uploaders, it will quite literally pay to increase your video's ratings—the number of views each video receives. Which leads to one of the questions I get asked most frequently: How do I increase the viewership of my YouTube videos?

Unfortunately, there's no short and simple answer to this question. Creating a must-see YouTube video requires a combination of appealing content, widespread exposure, and serendipity. There's no magic formula.

Content Is King

In Chapter 7, " What Type of Videos Do *You* Want to Upload?," we discussed what makes a great YouTube video. Without repeating that advice, know that for a video to really take off in terms of number of views, it has to have some combination of the following features:

- Unique
- Newsworthy
- Entertaining
- Professional

Home movies of your cat sitting on the toilet will prove only so popular. To attract widespread notice, your video has to have widespread appeal—and stand out from the millions of other videos on the YouTube site. When you produce that kind of content, people will pay attention—and you'll start getting exposure outside of YouTube, on other websites, and in the traditional media.

Exposure Is Everything

Exposure creates more exposure. The more people who view your video, the more people they'll share it with. And if you happen to get exposure outside of YouTube, things can really take off. (How many times have you seen YouTube videos on cable news shows—or late-night talk fests?)

It's worth your while to promote your video in as many different ways as possible. This can include any or all of the following:

- Embedding your video in your own blog or website
- Linking to your video in comments you make to other blogs
- Posting links to your video in other online forums and newsgroups
- Emailing links to your video to interested parties (not just friends and family)

You can also gain exposure by participating in the YouTube community. It pays to subscribe to a lot of YouTube channels, leave comments on as many videos as you can, and otherwise make a name for yourself with other YouTubers. The more people who see your name in comments and channels, the more people who'll link back to your channel and videos. What goes around comes around.

Luck Counts

When it comes to creating a truly viral video, there's only so much you can do. A lot of popular videos result from nothing more than pure luck. You're in the right place at the right time to record a newsworthy video, and then you're fortunate enough to have a TV station or cable channel take notice and broadcast the video to a large mainstream audience. You can't plan for serendipity. Do the best you can do, and let the nature of YouTube's video sharing take it the rest of the way.

15

Getting More Out of YouTube—With Third-Party Tools

YouTube is a feature-rich website—so feature-rich, in fact, that it's sometimes difficult to find everything that there is to be found. This has led to a variety of third-party tools and services, all designed to help you get even more out of YouTube than you can from the basic site.

Indexing YouTube Content

To me, one of the most annoying things about YouTube is finding the best content. There's a lot of chaff out there among the wheat, and it's often hard to separate one from the other.

To that end, several websites have been created to index YouTube content. These sites organize YouTube videos by various criteria—typically by popularity or buzzworthiness.

The most popular of these YouTube index sites include

- **Best of YouTube** (www.thebestofyoutube.com)—A blog that lists the current user-selected "best" (not necessarily the most popular) YouTube videos

- **IndexTube** (www.indextube.com)—Shown in Figure 15.1, a Wikipedia-like site that organizes videos from YouTube and other sites into easily navigated categories—music videos, TV shows, comedy, sports, and education

Figure 15.1
Browse YouTube videos by category at IndexTube.

- **SaneScreen** (www.sanescreen.com)—A user-edited directory of web-based videos

- **Top YouTube Videos** (www.topyoutubevideos.com)—A collection of the most popular and most buzzworthy YouTube videos

- **VideoRemote** (www.video-remote.com/)—Organizes videos on YouTube and other sites by category: television shows, cartoons, anime, and movies

- **Vidspedia** (www.vidspedia.com)—A categorized collection of the best clips from YouTube and other video sharing sites

- **Viral Video Chart** (www.viralvideochart.com)—Shown in Figure 15.2, tracks the top 20 most-blogged-about videos on the Web

■ **The World Internet TV Charts** (www.worldtv.com/charts/)—
Tracks the most popular videos on YouTube and other video
sharing sites

■ **YouTube Top-Rated** (www.coverpop.com/pop/youtube/)—
Shown in Figure 15.3, a "coverpop" with the 1,001 top-rated
YouTube videos; hover over any thumbnail image to view more
info and click to view the video

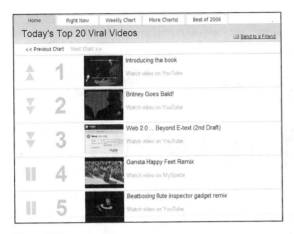

Figure 15.2
View the Web's most-blogged-about videos at Viral Video Chart.

Figure 15.3
View a "coverpop" of YouTube's top-rated videos at YouTube Top-Rated.

Automating YouTube Operations

Then there are the utilities and sites that help you automate various YouTube operations. These include

■ **MemoriesOnWeb** (www.codejam.com/slideshow/mow.htm)— Shown in Figure 15.4, a free program that creates video slideshows from your digital photos and then uploads the video to YouTube

Figure 15.4
Create photo slideshow videos with the MemoriesOnWeb program.

■ **Overstream** (www.overstream.net)—A site that lets you "mod" YouTube videos by adding your own subtitles

■ **Search The Tube** (www.searchthetube.com)—A search site for YouTube videos

■ **TvTube** (web.mac.com/netao/iWeb/TvTube%20Help/ Welcome.html)—A Macintosh software program that lets you create a library of clips from YouTube and other video sharing sites

- **YouTube CrazyVideos** (www.instaladordecontenidos.com/indexEn.php)—A free Windows program that lets you search YouTube and then play back videos in a desktop viewer

- **YouTube UserScripts** (www.userscripts.org/tag/youtube)—A collection of scripts that perform various YouTube tasks, including downloading YouTube videos, collecting links to YouTube videos, and so on (recommended for technically adept users only)

- **YouTube Video Slideshow** (www.yvoschaap.com/youtube/single.php)—A website that lets you play back all the YouTube videos by a given user or all the videos with a given tag with a single click

- **YouTube Widget** (www.apple.com/downloads/dashboard/movie_tv/youtubewidget.html)—Another Mac-only utility that lets you search YouTube videos from the Mac Dashboard

Info 4U — Want to cheat your way to higher page views for your YouTube videos? Then check out YouCheater ($10, cheatyoutube.awardspace.com), a software program that purports to generate up to 9,700 fake views per hour. Use your best judgment before purchasing.

Alternatives to YouTube: Other Video Sharing Sites

Finally, it's worth noting that although YouTube is the largest video sharing site on the Web, it isn't the only one. Several other sites let users upload and view videos at no charge, just like YouTube. Here are some of the more popular of these alternative video sharing sites:

- **AOL UnCut Video** (uncutvideo.aol.com)—Part of the larger AOL Video site, specializing in user-submitted videos

- **Break.com** (www.break.com)—Pays users if videos are featured on the site's home page

- **Dailymotion** (www.dailymotion.com)—Video sharing with tags and groups

- **eyespot** (www.eyespot.com)—In addition to hosting user-submitted videos, offers online tools for editing home videos

■ **FileCabi.net** (www.filecabi.net)—Specializing in unique and often bizarre videos

■ **Flixya** (www.flixya.com)—Video sharing with revenue sharing

■ **Footie Tube** (www.footie-tube.com)—Nothing but football (soccer) clips

■ **Google Video** (video.google.com)—YouTube's sister site in the Google empire, with a mix of commercial and user-submitted videos, as shown in Figure 15.5

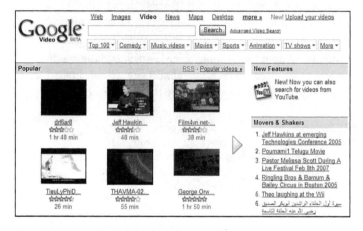

Figure 15.5
YouTube's sister site, Google Video.

■ **Grouper** (www.grouper.com)—Similar in features to YouTube

■ **GUBA** (www.guba.com)—Offers a mix of paid and free videos

■ **iFilm** (www.ifilm.com)—User-submitted videos and short independent films, organized by channel

■ **Joost** (www.joost.com)—Video sharing with tons of official videos from major media companies, including Viacom; offers a cool translucent interface for its videos, as shown in Figure 15.6

 Some industry analysts think that Joost will become YouTube's primary competitor, especially as several media companies have signed content distribution agreements with the site—while simultaneously pulling their videos from YouTube.

Figure 15.6
YouTube's highest-tech competitor, Joost.

- **Jumpcut** (www.jumpcut.com)—Video uploads and online "remixes"

- **LiveLeak** (www.liveleak.org)—Focusing on user-submitted news and reality videos

- **Metacafe** (www.metacafe.com)—Video sharing with a producer rewards program ($5 per 1,000 views)

- **Myubo** (www.myubo.com)—Video sharing via the Web and on your mobile phone

- **Ourmedia** (www.ourmedia.org)—Video, audio, and photo file sharing

- **Revver** (www.revver.com)—Video sharing with revenue sharing

- **Sharkle** (www.sharkle.com)—Similar to YouTube in features

- **Stage6** (stage6.divx.com)—A general video sharing site, hosted by DivX

- **Twango** (www.twango.com)—Video, audio, and photo sharing

- **VideoEgg** (www.videoegg.com)—Basic video sharing

- **Vimeo** (www.vimeo.com)—Another basic video sharing site
- **vMIX** (www.vmix.com)—Free video and music sharing, as shown in Figure 15.7

Figure 15.7
vMIX, one of many similar video sharing sites.

- **vSocial** (www.vsocial.com)—Yet another basic video sharing site
- **ZippyVideos** (www.zippyvideos.com)—More video sharing

 Looking to view and share adult videos online? Then check out PornoTube (www.pornotube.com) and XTube (www.xtube.com), two X-rated video sharing sites.

16

Troubleshooting YouTube Problems

For most users on most days, using YouTube is a snap. On rare occasions, however, something goes wrong, and you either can't play or upload a given video.

Fortunately, most YouTube problems are easy to diagnose and just as easy to fix. Read on to learn how to troubleshoot the most common YouTube problems.

Playback Problems

Proper playback of YouTube videos requires that you have the Adobe Flash software installed on your PC and that you're connected to a broadband (not dial-up) Internet connection. Failing to meet either of these two requirements accounts for most—but not all—YouTube playback problems.

That said, let's look at some of the most common problems you might encounter with YouTube playback.

Videos Won't Play

The number-one cause for videos not playing is that you don't have the latest version of the Adobe Flash Player (formerly Macromedia Flash Player) software installed on your PC. To download the latest version of the Flash Player (it's free), go to www.adobe.com/products/flashplayer/. You may need to reboot your computer following the installation.

 Even if you have (or think you have) the Flash Player installed on your system, it may not be the latest version. It's worth downloading and installing the latest version, just in case.

If you have the latest version of the Flash Player installed but still can't play back videos, you may have JavaScript turned off in your web browser; YouTube requires JavaScript for its video playback. In Internet Explorer 7, you can turn this back on by selecting Tools, Internet Options to display the Internet Options dialog box. Select the Security tab and then click the Custom Level button; when the Security Settings dialog box appears, scroll to the Scripting section and select the Enable options for both the Active Scripting and Scripting of Java Applets settings.

You may also need to lower the video acceleration on your computer, as some video content may need lower acceleration to play properly. To lower the hardware acceleration on a Windows XP PC, open the Windows Control Panel, select Appearance & Themes, Display, Settings, Advanced, Troubleshoot, Hardware Acceleration, and make the appropriate changes from there. (In Windows Vista, the path is Control Panel, Personalization, Display Settings, Advanced Settings, Troubleshoot, Change Settings.)

Videos Won't Play—QuickTime Logo Displayed

If you try to play a video and it not only doesn't play but also displays the QuickTime logo on top of the video player, you've accidentally selected QuickTime as your default Flash player, which it shouldn't be. You'll need to reconfigure QuickTime accordingly, which you do by opening the QuickTime Player application and selecting Edit,

Preferences, QuickTime Preferences to display the QuickTime dialog box. Select the Browser tab, click the MIME Settings button, and then uncheck the Miscellaneous option. Click OK to apply the changes, and then reboot your computer.

Videos Get Hung Up on the Loading Screen

When your videos start to load but then seem to get stuck on the initial screen, you could have one of a number of different problems.

First, make sure you're connected to a broadband Internet connection of at least 500Kbps. Anything less can cause YouTube videos to freeze like this.

Second, you could have a pop-up blocker (for your web browser) blocking the incoming video stream. Try disabling your browser's pop-up blocker to allow the incoming stream.

Third, your computer's firewall utility could also be blocking the incoming video. Try reconfiguring your firewall to allow incoming video from the YouTube site.

It's also possible that you have another streaming video program running at the same time, and the two programs are competing with each other for your computer's attention. Make sure you've closed Windows Media Player, the QuickTime Player, and similar programs before you try to watch YouTube videos.

Finally, make sure you're not trying to watch a private YouTube video. Unlike normal public videos, YouTube's private videos are restricted for viewing by invited contacts only. Try to play a private video, and, unless you're on the guest list, nothing will happen.

Playback Stops and Starts, or Stutters

Poor playback is typically caused by a single factor—a slow Internet connection. Dial-up connections are particularly problematic and can even cause the incoming video stream to freeze. A long-term solution to this problems is to upgrade to a faster broadband Internet connection; best performance comes from a connection speed of at least 500Kbps.

That said, broadband Internet connections can also cause problems, especially during busy times of the day or if you're trying to download large files or pictures simultaneously with your YouTube viewing. It's also possible that YouTube itself has some slow server problems; again, this tends to happen during the busiest times of the day. Wait a few minutes for the traffic to decrease and then try viewing the video again.

No Audio with the Video

If you play a YouTube video and there's no accompanying audio, first check to see whether you hear audio with other YouTube videos; it's always possible that the person who uploaded the video screwed up and forgot to attach an audio track.

If none of your YouTube videos have sound, check the volume controls both in the YouTube player and on your computer. Make sure your computer speakers (or a set of earphones) are connected, that the volume is cranked up, and that you haven't accidentally muted the sound. If worse comes to worst, reboot your computer and try again.

Videos End Before They're Done

This is an odd problem that sometimes crops up. You're watching a video, and in the middle somewhere the video just stops and shows the end screen.

The cause of this problem is typically a bad copy of the video previously downloaded to your PC. When a download is incomplete, the truncated version of the video file sometimes gets stuck on your hard disk—and then it's this copy of the video that is played by YouTube, and that causes the problem.

To solve this problem, you need to clear your web browser's cache or temporary files. In Internet Explorer 7, this is done by clicking Tools, Delete Browser History, and then clicking the Delete Files button.

You Click a Link to a YouTube Video but Nothing Happens

This is caused by a bad link. (Sometimes YouTube will even display an error message to that effect, or that the URL contained a "malformed

video ID.") This happens when someone types a video link URL manually and enters a typo. If this someone was you, go back and copy
and paste the correct link to the video.

You Click a Link to a YouTube Video but the Video Has Been Removed

This happens, and it's not your fault. Even live links on the YouTube
site sometimes point to videos that have been removed for terms of
use (typically copyright) violations, or have been taken down volun-
tarily by the videos' owners. If you see a message that says a video is
no longer available, that's why.

Uploading Problems

Not all YouTube problems are playback-related. You can also run into
trouble when you're uploading a video. Here are some of the most
common upload-related problems.

It's Taking a Long Time to Upload the Video

Be patient; the longer your video is, the longer it will take to upload.
Depending on the size of your upload and the speed of your Internet
connection, it might take several hours for the video to be completely uploaded. If it takes more than a few hours, especially for a
shorter video, try canceling the upload and starting over again.

You Try to Upload a Video but Receive an "Invalid File Format" Message

This happens when you try to upload a video file that is in a file
format that YouTube doesn't accept. You'll need to convert your video
to either .AVI, .MOV, .MPG, or .WMV file formats. (And, even though
YouTube converts your files to .FLV format, you can't upload an
.FLV-format file. Go figure.)

If you have your video in the right file format, it's possible you've
used the wrong video compression codec. YouTube recommends
saving your videos in the MPEG-4 format with either the DivX or
XviD codec.

You Try to Upload a Video but Receive an "Unable to Convert Video File" Message

This is a similar error message to the one discussed previously and is caused by the same problem—you tried to upload a video in an unaccepted file format. Convert your video to an acceptable file format before you upload it again.

You Try to Upload a Video but Receive an "Empty .MOV File" Message

This error message tells you that your upload failed because you tried to upload the wrong QuickTime file. When you save a movie from the QuickTime Player with the Save as a Reference Movie option selected, QuickTime creates a small .MOV file that points to the larger full-length video file located elsewhere on your hard drive. If you accidentally try to upload the smaller pointer file, YouTube objects, because that file doesn't contain actual video content. You'll need to re-save the movie from within the QuickTime Player, this time with the Save as a Self-Contained Movie option selected, and then retry the upload to YouTube.

You Try to Upload a Video but the File Is Rejected as a Duplicate

When YouTube displays the "Rejected (Duplicate Upload)" message, that means you tried to upload a file that already exists on the YouTube site. YouTube checks the content of all files in its system (not the actual content, but rather the checksum of the video bits and bytes) to weed out duplicate videos. Know that simply renaming the file won't get around this limitation; you'll need to re-edit your video to make it somehow different from the existing file before you can complete the upload. (Or don't upload it, since someone else already did.)

You Try to Upload a File but It's Rejected for a Terms of Use Violation

When YouTube displays the "Rejected (Terms of Use Violation)" message, that means you've tried to upload a video that somehow violates YouTube's terms of use. Perhaps the video contains adult content, or maybe it infringes on someone else's copyright. Review YouTube's terms of use (www.youtube.com/t/terms) to see what you've done wrong.

The Audio and Video for Your Uploaded File Are Out of Sync

When a person in your video says one thing but something different comes out of his mouth, you have a sync problem. This is typically caused by the use of an audio codec not supported by YouTube. Try re-encoding your video using the standard MP3 audio codec.

Your Uploaded Video Looks Lousy

Assuming that your video looked good to begin with, there may be three causes for this problem.

First, you may have uploaded a video using the wrong file format, compression scheme, or codec. Remember, YouTube recommends the MPEG-4 format with either the DivX or XviD codec.

Second, if you uploaded a .MOV-format file, know that YouTube doesn't always do a good job converting this type of file to the site's native .FLV format. Try converting the .MOV file to .AVI, .MPG, or .WMV and uploading it again.

Finally, you may have uploaded a video with too large a picture— that is, too high a resolution. The higher the resolution, the more YouTube has to convert that file to a lower resolution—and YouTube's conversion process sometimes produces suck-worthy video quality. It's better for you to reduce the resolution of your video before you upload it; for best results, go for a 320×240 resolution.

Your Uploaded Video Doesn't Show Up When You Search YouTube

First, be patient, it can take 8 hours or more for a new video to show up in YouTube's search index. Second, check the tags you've applied to the video; look for misspellings or other problems that could affect search results. (And make sure you have tags; people can't find a video that doesn't have any tags applied!) Finally, make sure you've added your username as a tag, so that people searching for your videos by your name can find it.

Index

BOOKS ONLINE

ENABLED

THIS BOOK IS SAFARI ENABLED

INCLUDES FREE 45-DAY ACCESS TO THE ONLINE EDITION

The Safari® Enabled icon on the cover of your favorite technology book means the book is available through Safari Bookshelf. When you buy this book, you get free access to the online edition for 45 days.

Safari Bookshelf is an electronic reference library that lets you easily search thousands of technical books, find code samples, download chapters, and access technical information whenever and wherever you need it.

TO GAIN 45-DAY SAFARI ENABLED ACCESS TO THIS BOOK:

- Go to **http://www.quepublishing.com/safarienabled**
- Complete the brief registration form
- Enter the coupon code found in the front of this book on the "Copyright" page

If you have difficulty registering on Safari Bookshelf or accessing the online edition, please e-mail customer-service@safaribooksonline.com.